THE HEART OF A GRANDPARENT

Investing Yourself in Your Grandchildren's Future

Eric E. Wiggin

Harold Shaw Publishers
Wheaton, Illinois

ISBN 0-87788-368-8

Library of Congress Cataloging-in-Publication Data

Wiggin, Eric E.
   The heart of a grandparent / Investing yourself in your
grandchildren's future.
     p. cm.
   ISBN 0-87788-368-8
   1. Grandparenting—United States. 2. Grandparent and child—
United States. I. Title.
   HQ759.9.W54 1993
306.874'5—dc20   92-41163
                                     CIP

---

99 98 97 96 95 94 93

10 9 8 7 6 5 4 3 2 1

To the grandmothers of my children, Pauline Fuller Wiggin and Hattie Grissom Hackney, who have joyfully taken unto themselves the injunction to "Be fruitful and multiply." And to their more than 100 descendants at this writing, and to mine, who, when grandparents themselves may find joy, hope, and inspiration in the words on these pages.

E.E. Wiggin
Fruitport, Michigan
September 1992

Contents

1 Grandparenting Is "Absolutely Wonderful".........1

2 Around the Corner to Grandma's House...........11

3 Seeing through Your Grandchild's Eyes 29

4 The Extended Family: Yesterday and Today.....39

5 Grandfather's Mountain 51

6 When Grandmas and Grandpas Were Old 65

7 Things Not Found in Books 85

8 Busy Moms, Babysitting Grandmoms 99

9 The Split-Family Grandparent 111

10 Grandparents across the Miles 123

11 When Your Grandchild's Ears Fall Off 137

12 Who's That Boy with the Pimples?.................149

13 Grandparents Bearing Gifts.............................163

14 Parenting Is for Parents 175

15 Are Today's Kids Different? 187

16 When Love Must Say "No"..............................201

17 Investing in Your Grandchildren's Future.......217

18 Eternal Values 233

19 Letting Go without Losing Your Posterity 241

20 The Grandchild Who Climbs Trees.................253

1

Grandparenting Is "Absolutely Wonderful"

"We all think you're absolutely wonderful at the two most important kinds of fathering—regular and grand." This was the caption on a Father's Day card from my daughter Debbie, her husband, Lew, and my granddaughter, Katy. There is no "Grandfather's Day" on my calendar, but I don't mind. This past Father's Day I added two more who think I'm absolutely wonderful. It took eleven years to get the first four, my children. At the present rate I'll have twenty two more in the next eleven years, my grandchildren.

I'll admit I was anything but prepared to become a grandfather when it took me by storm, literally. At the time, a September Monday morning, I was in the living room of my son's apartment in Charleston, South Carolina at daybreak. My wife, Dot, and I had landed in Charleston the day after Hugo, one of the century's worst hurricanes, had come straight up Charleston Harbor on its way inland. Lines were down, and long-

1

distance calls were unthinkable, except for after midnight or very early in the morning.

But the phone rang. It was my mother in Indiana. Our daughter, Debbie, in Michigan, had just become a mother, making Dot and me grandparents. I dressed and went to the bathroom where I washed my face and combed my hair in the light of a wax candle. No use to consider the electric razor. Right then I decided to grow a beard.

Some grandpas have grey beards. Some are bald. Some, like myself, still have enough salt and pepper hair to comb. Some grandmas have white hair and sit in rockers and knit. Some have brown, black, red, or blonde hair; they jog, swim, and bike. Some grandparents are ninetysomething and live in nursing homes. A few are thirtysomething and busy with the stuff of daily living. Many are fortysomething, fiftysomething, or sixtysomething.

All grandparents have one thing in common: In a quieter, more profound way than when they first became parents, they have been brought face to face with their importance in the continuity of life. Some quickly looked away, trying to avoid their responsibility. Some have shrugged, frowned, and made fools of themselves by seeking their lost youth in the world's sullied fountains. Some, the grandparents to whom this book is written, have embraced their newfound responsibility and in God's grace have begun to fulfill it.

For the Christian grandparent, God has his special blessings in store. God's mercy and righteous dealings are extended from one generation to another, even to the grandchildren of the godly, David writes in Psalm 103:17-18. For instance, my grandparents were Christian believers who honored the Lord. Their grandchildren, myself included, have all been blessed, I believe, as a result.

Most folks conceive their notions of grandparents early in life. My own conception, which I'm sure is shared by many, was that grandparents were elderly, had grey hair, wore old-fashioned clothes and, if not feeble in the muscles were at least stiff in the joints. All grandparents seemed at least seventy; some appeared to be past ninety. And all that I knew had a musty, slightly Victorian air about them.

I had five grandparents, all born in the nineteenth century. When I was small, these grandparents still had fragments of their own families alive—aunts, uncles, cousins. My maternal grandmother's mother was still living, though I couldn't for the life of me figure out why two "old" ladies with steel grey hair were both called "Grandma" by me, but one (the one who did the housework) called the other "Mother." It didn't seem right somehow. My mother's mother was actually a prematurely grey fortysomething, but they both seemed the same age—and almost eternal.

My grandparents furnished our family with the basis for a happy Fourth of July reunion each summer. The family would gather on the lawn in front of Great Uncle Willie's barn, and the adults would spread planks on sawhorses for tables while brothers, sisters, and cousins took turns doing loop-the-loops in Uncle Willie's canvas hammock, stretched between two great maples by the gravel road. The celebration would end with homemade ice cream, frozen in hand-cranked freezers with ice from Father's ice house—there was no electricity in that corner of rural Maine in those days—then the family would return home to milk the cows and shoot Roman candles into the starry night.

The wheel of life has turned full circle since those halcyon celebrations dominated by my elders. In a span of some twenty years my great-grandmother and four grandparents died. The last leaf fell a quarter of a century ago, at age ninety-five, and I myself am now a grandparent four times over.

There are things I learned as a grandchild that I wish to pass on to my grandchildren as well as to pass across to other grandparents who may find them useful in their grandparenting. But, beyond the nostalgia, life has practical, important, valuable lessons.

Too, this book includes conversations with other grandparents, such as Jack Wyrtzen, founder and director of Word of Life, whose influence as a youth leader has reached millions and whose strength as a father and grandfather has touched several generations of Christian leaders. It contains talks with Jim Franks, founder of Concern International, who with his wife, Shirley, raised six children of their own, as well as three adopted Korean girls and a foster son, and chats with several lesser-known grandads and grandmas. Christian financial expert and director of Stewardship Services Foundation, Jim Rickard, shares about a grandparent and his money in this book. And Christian psychologist and author, Dr. Kevin Leman, talks about the effect of the mid-life crisis on grandparenting.

But the next several pages shall be devoted to lessons from the past, from my childhood when my grandparents were living. These vignettes will serve to introduce me and furnish a foundation for what is subsequently said.

◆

*Grandmas are
for adventures*

is one of the first lessons a child learns in early life. It was a September before I was old enough for school, and my dad had hired his bean thresher and tractor out to my grandmother's uncle. Dad and Mother worked together on the thresher, and Uncle Lew and his crew hauled the dry beans from the field.

Grandma Fuller took little brother George and me to the bean field in a baby carriage, then we went down the road to a plank bridge where she lifted us out. I knelt at the edge of the bridge to watch a frog hop from a rock and swim off down the brook. We left for the house, Grandma pushing the empty carriage, I happily holding her hand, and George toddling along clutching her long skirts.

Fun in simple pleasures builds bridges between the old and the very young that thoughtful grandparents will explore thoroughly. The grandparent who impacts his grandchild's life is the one who is willing to kneel down to the child's level, to laugh at what he or she laughs at, to cry at what makes him or her tearful. When I was small, I knew that Grandma could *feel* what I felt.

◆

*Grandpas can
do silly things.*

One winter evening I watched Grandpa Wiggin milk a cow in the light of a kerosene lantern. Out of the shadows came a half-grown kitten, and Grandpa took aim with the teat he was squeezing and squirted the kitty in her mug. One more shot of milk, this time over the kitten's head, and the hungry creature stood on its hind legs to reach, mouth wide open for the cow squeezings. Three or four squirts, and he had the kitten trained to reach for the milk whenever he called and took aim.

Cats learn fast. Grandpas are slow to forget. A silly trick he'd learned three quarters of a century earlier as a kid would still entertain a child. Yet in retrospect, my grandfather was not being silly. He had learned that the action-reaction of a stream of milk and a stretching cat would build a bridge into the heart of a grandchild.

◆

*Grandparents are
sometimes thoughtless.*

Great-grandmother had been a school teacher, and she had committed to memory "Little Orphant Annie" by "The Hoosier Schoolmaster," James Whitcomb Riley. I was spending the night with Great-grandmother and Grandma and Grandpa Fuller, and just at bedtime Great-grandmother, Grandma Fuller's mother, quoted me this poem with the lines about the "Little boy who wouldn't say his prayers" who was "put to bed away upstairs" where "his mammy heerd him holler an' his daddy heerd him bawl" and "when they pulled the kivers back he wasn't there at all" for "the gobble-uns'll gitcha ef yuh don't watch out."

Grandma Fuller put me to bed away upstairs right after that. You can be sure I said my prayers that night. Grandparents sometimes fail to consider childish emotions when they repeat things they may consider amusing or cute.

◆

*Grandmas
can be tough.*

Grandma Wiggin was a tall woman with broad hips and long, strong arms. She moved with Victorian dignity, but she wouldn't hesitate to wrestle her heavy pressure canner off her hot, wood-fired range and carry it loaded across her country kitchen to the sink. Mother, a small woman, couldn't do that, even though she could pitch bean vines into a threshing machine. Although a child may exaggerate his grandparents' frailties, he may all the same be awed by a grandparent's abilities, which can seem almost superhuman.

◆

*Grandpas are
very wise.*

My grandfathers knew everything and they had done everything—or at least everything anybody could wish to know or do. Grandpa Fuller had been a Boston street-car conductor at the turn of the century, and he had once seen Jimmy Durante in a vaudeville show in Boston. He had watched Harry Houdini locked into an iron box and lowered through the ice of the Charles River. Grandpa Wiggin had helped his father clear stump-filled pastures to make the fields that were later Father's farm. Before mowing machines he had cut hay with a hand scythe and carted it to the barn with his oxen, stubborn creatures who once spent the night on a pile of hay rather than cross a boggy hayfield.

So when my grandfathers argued politics during the Presidential election of '52—these two men who knew so much—I sat thrilled on the edge of my chair taking it all in. Grandpa Fuller was a Taft Republican and Grandpa Wiggin was an Eisenhower man.

One of the greatest thrills of my life (I was thirteen in 1952) was to sit up late with Grandpa Wiggin and listen to the election returns on his radio. He "liked Ike." So did both my grandpas by then. Children admire the wisdom and knowledge of grandparents whom they love. In later life such influences often have a profound effect on adult decisions and actions.

◆

*Grandparents
are forever.*

Like Melchizedek, a small child's grandparents have "neither beginning of days nor end of life" (Hebrews 7:3). Though I was eight when Great-grandmother died, this did not affect me seriously. We had not been close, for she had sat in the shadows of my grandmother's kitchen, seldom venturing from her platform rocker when children were around.

But my four grandparents always had been and always would be, it seemed then. They were constant. They were predictable. Grandpa Fuller had always been a storekeeper and a part-time sheriff (though he sometimes told other worldly tales of his youth in Boston). Grandpa Wiggin had lived much of his eighty-some years farming the same farm where he grew up. Only later did I learn that he had also been a mail carrier, a mill hand, and for a time a school superintendent, and in his middle years a prominent member of our community.

I was in my fourteenth year when Grandpa Wiggin died, and he in his eighty-fifth. I remember well the raw January forenoon when he took sick with pneumonia. He was splitting wood and I was tossing it into the shed. Grandpa began to spit blood, and I was scared.

Then came the day Grandpa died. With a shock I learned something new: grandparents are not forever. They are given by God to appreciate while we can.

Yet the presence of one or more grandparents in a child's life helps him put into mature perspective the importance as well as the brevity of his own existence. This maturing process requires that an individual understand and respect the relationship between the three great phases of life: childhood, adulthood, old age. Today's youth-centered culture has, sadly, lost even its ability to mature.

We who are grandparents have been given to our grandchildren to aid in their development for what years we may have left. Some of us will see the first of our grandchildren grow to maturity, have children of their own, and start the cycle over again. Some of us may not have that privilege. Some of us have grandchildren nearby. Others, in this American culture where families move once every five years and young families more often than that, must do much of our grandparenting by phone, mail, or tape recording. Or we may become surrogate grandparents for the grandchildren of others.

Whatever our case, our tasks are alike: to seek the glory of God in the lives of our grandchildren as we model Christ before them.

2

Around the Corner to Grandma's House

Grandma's kitchen always smelled of baking bread, beans, and molasses cookies, fresh from the oven. And Grandma didn't complain if you took one without asking—or more than one!

"There's milk in the fridge to go with the cookies," Grandma would say as she bent to stir the beans. If you spilled your milk on the tablecloth, Grandma merely murmured, "Never mind; I'll mop it up"—and she did, without complaining. She didn't tell you to close the door, either. Grandma treated you like a human being, not like a number in a herd.

Grandma never yelled at you. Not once. Grandma was unhurried, so she had time to appreciate you as an individual.

Grandma's House was quiet, so quiet that, if you think about it, you can even now hear the hum of her refrigerator with its top-mounted compressor. And, after the refrigerator shut off with a shudder that made the dishes rattle, you could hear the cat purring in Grandma's kitchen rocker.

Grandma's House was a haven from the shrill competition of siblings, from the stern corrections of parents, from the sullen cares that crowd into the life of even a child. Grandma's House, whether over the river and through the woods—as in the days of long ago—or just a tricycle ride around the corner of an urban neighborhood, was almost heaven.

Grandma's House of thirty or fifty years ago didn't have the sterile smell of air freshener and new carpeting found in today's homes. If Grandma had a wood- or coal-fired range, common in many rural or village homes as recently as about 1950, her kitchen smelled of oak or pine or coal smoke. On the back of her range simmered a pan of sweet apples, picked from the gnarled old tree just outside her kitchen door, which in summer was open to let fresh breezes waft through the screen.

In winter, spring, or fall, Grandma's kitchen was the coziest place on earth. But the rest of the year her kitchen was hot, except in early morning. But no mind; on those days you ate at an old table set up on the back porch.

Grandma kept a box of toys under the stairs that you could have all to yourself without having to share. There were cast-iron enameled autos to push on the floor, a battered old bisque doll, and an Erector set. You saw one of those dolls in an antique shop recently, and you're not sure whether you were moved more by memories of Grandma's House or by the price: nearly $1,000!

When the evening supper dishes were cleared away, Grandma brought out a box of board games. There were backgammon, checkers, and Parcheesi. Chinese checkers and maybe even a Monopoly game with no missing pieces were in Grandma's old wooden soap box. And at Grandma's you always stayed up to finish the game, no matter how late. At Grandma's House bedtime was whenever you couldn't keep your eyes open any longer.

Breakfast came at Grandma's House later than at home, for Grandma was never in a hurry to go anywhere. You got up to the smell of hot biscuits, and when you came downstairs you discovered that Grandma had already been to the garden to pick fresh raspberries for breakfast.

You can add your own memories of Grandma's House to those mentioned here. You are a grandmother or a grandfather now. And these memories furnish a starting point for preparing your own house to receive grandchildren.

Children, whether yesterday or today, need the solace of Grandma's sanctuary to develop into full-rounded adults. A grandmother can do many things to make her house special for her grandchildren. As a grandmother, new or experienced, you honor Christ by seeking ways to make your home a place your grandchildren will remember in the latter years of their lives.

◆

Make physical preparations for
these special guests, your grandchildren.
This may mean a high chair, a crib in the
guest room, and perhaps such items as a potty
chair, a stroller, and a child's car seat. Sooner or
later you will probably need a playpen.

But you've shot your wad of pin money on baby clothes, a shower, and perhaps a plane ticket to see your daughter or daughter-in-law with her precious bundle. And last year you gave that family heirloom crib in the attic to your niece. How can you now afford to supply your *own* nursery?

It's time you discovered yard/garage sales! For openers, nobody expects you to have *new* equipment on hand for occasional use by young guests. With the aid of a newspaper you can discover half a dozen pieces of serviceable baby furniture or equipment for a fraction of their new cost for sale by mothers whose toddlers are now grown. Pass up the broken, dilapidated stuff and look for the best. It might be unwise to buy old items for a new mother, though, but for your own use used equipment may be exactly what you need.

Look for toys and books appropriate to the needs of your grandchildren. These should be chosen with an eye to keeping the child occupied with a minimum of supervision, and the simple ones are best. A book of 100 or so dot-to-dot puzzles, for example, will fascinate most children with the dexterity to trace a line with a crayon or pencil. Push toys, such as trucks, tractors, and autos for back-yard or sand-box play will entertain for hours. A doll and a stuffed animal or two will please the under-ten set, and the animals are all the more appreciated if you give them names!

If you wish to branch out, tricycles and bicycles of all description are to be found in yard sales. These will keep your older grandchildren from feeling stranded at their home away from home. Swing sets and sand boxes are sometimes found in yard sales as well.

There are toys appropriate only for Dennis the Menace or Bart Simpson, however. Though slingshots, bows and arrows, or air rifles (BB guns) sometimes have their place with developing children under parental supervision, you are not depriving your grandchild by refusing to let him or her bring hazardous toys on a weekend visit. A pocket knife would be okay if the child is used to carrying one, but a bow can send arrows into your neighbor's yard! One young teen, reared in a suburban subdivision, visited his grandparents who lived on a rural road. Here he set up his pup tent and with his .22-caliber rifle terrorized the neighbors for some days until he wounded his grandfather's dog. Children placed in an unaccustomed environment often behave in inappropriate ways.

Sports equipment also should be purchased with caution. You may wish, for example, to restrict the child to soft balls (e.g. softballs, soccer balls, rubber balls); no hard balls, such as baseballs or golf balls, since these often break windows unless used under closer supervision than you may be ready to supply.

Your choice of toys will vary with your circumstances, of course. The grandparent who owns a 500-acre Nebraska ranch can be more liberal than one who lives in a New York apartment. If grandparents own a farm, it might be okay to let a twelve-year-old grandson fire Grandpa's 12-gauge (under adult supervision, of course).

◆

*Make your
home safe.*

Toddlers, for instance, can fall down stairs so stairs need gates. If Grandpa owns hunting guns, they must never, ever be left loaded, and preferably they should be in a locked cabinet. Many adults, grown accustomed to living in a home without small children, fail to realize the serious potential of even the common, seemingly harmless habit of leaving one's keys in the car for a few minutes. Toddlers have turned keys on, slipped the car into neutral, and coasted it into the street or over another child—or frightened, have jumped out and fallen under the moving vehicle themselves.

Most grandparents are aware of the dangers presented by medicines and cleaning chemicals which could kill or seriously harm a child. A locked cabinet, or at the least one out of reach of toddlers, is mandatory. Keyed locks can be fitted onto wooden kitchen cupboards by anyone handy with tools. A garage cabinet can easily be supplied with a hasp and a padlock.

Speaking of garages, did you know that anti-freeze tastes sweet, like a delicious punch? It comes in child-resistant containers, true enough. But a lot of folks, like myself, mix it 50/50 with water, then put the extra gallon in a plastic milk jug! Be sure that that jug is in a locked car trunk or an inaccessible garage cabinet, if the grandchildren are coming to call.

A lot of grandparents, especially grandads, own expensive, tempting adult toys. A friend of mine lost a grandson, a child of about six, when he fell into a mowing machine while riding behind Grandpa on the tractor seat. Another grandfather took his fifteen-year-old grandson, who could drive a car, for a ride in his single-engine airplane. He showed the boy how the controls worked and even let him try flying. The teen had access to the plane's keys and later tried to fly alone. He got the airplane airborne, then landed—nose-down.

◆

Make your home
comfortable for children.

This will require some compromise, to be sure. If your living room is supplied with a white carpet, Chippendale furniture, fine porcelain lamps, and cut glass vases it may be best to make the living room off limits to all but adults who remove their shoes. This *may* work *if* your living room can be shut off from the rest of the house without seriously disrupting the household traffic flow and you have a family room with ceiling lighting and a dark-pattern tweed carpet to hide the dirt. Otherwise, put the breakables out of reach, temporarily install a plastic runner across the carpet, and resort to frequent washings to keep your grandchildren's hands as pure as you imagine their hearts to be.

◆

Provide suitable overnight
accommodations for your grandkids.

This may not require the bunk beds you used when your own children were small. Creative planning can result in some delightfully unusual arrangements. One family with a farm has a rustic cottage tucked away in the woods on a stream half a mile back where the grand-children and married children can vacation. Others with smaller spreads can let the grandkids set up a tent in the back yard. Many communities permit householders with large lots to park camping trailers in the yard for two weeks to a month at a time. Such privileges should be taken advantage of only where the neighbors don't mind, of course, and only in suburban or small village loca-tions where there is no danger of prowlers.

Usually, however, most grandparents find a simple solution in redecorating what was once a child's bed-room as a guest room, and then furnish it with a double bed, a dresser, and perhaps a crib. When the married children come to call they get the guest room and the kids sleep on a fold-out bed in the family room or in sleeping bags on foam pads, or even on the back porch, if it's warm weather.

When your grandchild visits alone, he or she gets the luxury of "the big bed" all to himself. How well I remember my own childhood experiences at my grandparents, whose nineteenth-century home, formerly a country inn, had never been wired for electricity above the ground floor. Grandma would accompany me upstairs where the double bed in the back bedroom was cozy with flannel sheets and a hot soapstone from the oven of her wood-fired kitchen range. Grandma carried matches and I a flashlight. She lit the lamp on the dresser, and after prayers were said and I was tucked in—feet firmly planted on the hot-towel-swaddled soapstone—she then blew out the lamp and left me with a flashlight under my pillow. I felt princely grand yet terribly alone during those nights upstairs in that old inn.

An advantage grandparents have over parents is that they can decide how many grandchildren can stay at once and for how long without being accused of cruelty. My own grandmother, though she occasionally would babysit my siblings and me, never permitted but one grandchild to visit overnight at a time. Such an arrangement has the obvious advantage of enabling Grandma to keep her sanity. More important, these are tremendous opportunities for a child to have the one-on-one attention of a loving adult, an experience today not often realized by many children, except first and only children.

*Lay in a supply
of kid food.*

You may subsist on minute steaks. Your active grandson may prefer macaroni and cheese—lots of it! It's certainly futile to try to change a child's (wretched?!) eating habits in the week he's your house guest, and you'll only make yourself and the child miserable if you don't cater to *some* of his eating habits, at least.

Crackers and peanut butter will keep most kids happy for between-meal snacks, and peanut butter is nutritious. (Despite what the TV ads say, few children can tell the difference between the cheap stuff and the high-priced spread.) Homemade cookies, cakes, and pies will make them happier still, along with giving you a sense of satisfaction in creative cooking. A really resourceful grandma will be long remembered for cooking her grandchildren's favorite dish.

◆

*Use visits for an opportunity
for cousins to visit each other.*

This must be done with a judicious concern for compatibility, however. Since one purpose of grandparenting is to aid a child to develop as an individual rather than as a member of the herd, as happens in school and day-care settings and far too commonly in the home, it is my feeling that cousins or siblings should not be invited to share the grandparents' time if they are going to compete for attention. This may sometimes be avoided by inviting cousins with no competing interests; for example, a teen girl who helps Grandma with the housework may also entertain an eight-year-old cousin, and each enjoys the companionship of the grandparents on his or her own level.

The Mutt and Jeff approach—an older child and a small one—to pairing grandkids when they visit may help solve the problem of not enough weekends or summer vacation days to go around. Some grandparents may have only two or three grandchildren. But we know one lady, age eighty-four, who has a descendant for every year of her life—children, grandchildren, great-grandchildren, and great-great-grandchildren. Most of them live nearby and treat her home as their second home. "Mom, come get me; I stopped at Grandma's after going fishing," is a frequent phone plaint her daughters and married granddaughters hear—I know; I'm the grandfather of four of her great-grandchildren!

Holidays are exceptions to the one grandchild or Mutt and Jeff rule, of course. And this requires special attention to the needs of the children *and* the needs of grandparents. Some grandmothers will insist on cooking Thanksgiving dinner for the entire brood until, after years of toil and a middling amount of enjoyment, the daughters and daughters-in-law finally protest that they are themselves now grandmothers and will Mother

(Great-grandmother!) please allow them to have their own family celebrations, to which she is of course invited.

The aged matriarch mentioned has found a creative solution to this dilemma that enables her to continue to express her mothering instincts, enjoy her extended family, and give her descendants a memorable Christmas. She gave up on Thanksgiving a dozen years ago, when her brood was no longer able to crowd around her table, even in successive seatings. A few years later she similarly quit cooking for Christmas dinner, eating instead with a daughter who is a grandmother.

But this grandame starts Christmas breakfast at six o'clock with the aid of a daughter. A merry, constantly changing crowd of children and adults climb over each other for the next four hours, feasting on bacon, sausage, eggs, and biscuits. Then the paper plates are whisked away, daughters do the dishes, and Great-great-grandma is bundled off to spend the rest of the day (which includes a long nap!) with one of her many families. These Christmas breakfasts will be remembered as a family highlight long after she passes on to her reward.

◆

*Find special ways to
entertain your grandchildren.*

Entertainment need not require the grandparents' full time, however, and it will necessarily be limited by whether either or both grandparents are employed and by the length of the stay.

The simplest is an overnight stay. My own stays with my grandparents usually began on Saturday afternoon, and I had entertainment enough for several hours watching my grandparents wait on customers in the small grocery store in the wing of their house. Grandpa was a part-time sheriff on call Saturday evening, and my encounter with him on such evenings was the thrill of seeing him dressed in his business suit, his silver badge discreetly pinned inside his coat, stride off to keep order at the local dance hall. "Be careful, Will," Grandma would warn in worried tones, and my excited imagination ran wild as I considered what daring use he might make of the handcuffs he dropped into his coat pocket on his way out the door. If I returned with my parents after Sunday school for dinner the next day, I often heard Grandpa regale us with tales of troublemakers he'd tossed out or even hauled off to jail.

Alone with Grandma for the evening, I'd listen to radio operas such as "Amos 'n' Andy" or "Inner Sanctum" while she did the supper dishes. Then we'd play checkers or backgammon until bedtime. It was my thrill to occasionally beat Grandma at checkers!

Today, the TV set is the handiest form of entertainment ever invented—and since the Roman gladiator games, probably the worst. If you are going to offer your grandchild worthwhile experiences, it will often be necessary to forego your favorite show and pay attention to *him*.

For openers, you *could* try checkers or another board game. Special seasonal events, such as fairs and plays, are occasions your grandchild will long remember. Boys and girls from stroller size through early teens enjoy zoos and picnic lunches, for instance.

Try to think of unique events not available to your grandchild in his home town, and plan to enjoy these together. A grandmother in Fort Wayne, Indiana sometimes invites grandchildren for a weekend in November or December, then takes them for a tour of the reconstruction of the colonial Old Fort Wayne, with room after room of folks in period costume celebrating Christmas in the traditions of European settlers in early wilderness America as they answer visitors' questions. City dwelling grandparents have access to museums, theaters, and interesting stores and malls to thrill the grandchildren. Country grandparents have simpler, but nevertheless interesting entertainments to create memories for their grandchildren. A visit to an agricultural fair can coincide with a grandchild's week with his farm-dwelling grandparents, for instance.

◆

Entertaining teens and young adults
can be trying—or a pleasure!

And the experience can be even more interesting if you raised only girls or only boys and the grandchild is the other sex.

In case you've forgotten from raising your own children, a teenager is essentially an immature adult. He or she has the desires, ambitions, and appetites of an adult and many of the abilities. Your teen grandchild can probably drive a car, and your grandson may be fairly competent at repairing one; your teen granddaughters can tend babies—and give birth to babies! Teens can discuss politics, spiritual matters, or sex with adult-like perception. Teens can take care of their own physical needs: they can dress themselves, shave, and curl their hair; they can cook and do laundry. They may also leave the dishes undone and the bed unmade unless you gently remind them that you could use some help. A weekend with a teen can be a pleasure or a pain, and you, Grandma and Grandpa, the mature members of the group, can be the catalysts to make the difference.

Young people who visit their grandparents, with few exceptions, do so because they want—often very badly—the companionship of their elders. The same grandmother who beat me at checkers when I was nine became a friend in whom I could confide when I was nineteen. She wrote me letters, long and full of family news. When I came home from college, we talked. And you know what? Grandma wanted to listen to me! I soon found that she was fascinated with what I had to say, and she had more time to listen than did my parents.

It's taken me a few years to sort out the reasons why Grandma had such an interest in me, but now a grandfather myself, I think I know. First, Grandma was an only child raised by a widowed mother, so boys and men were not a large part of her early life. She married my grandfather at twenty-two, he being thirty-seven. He was not a Christian until shortly before his death, so there was little spiritual communication between them. Their children were both girls. I think my mother's parents both saw me as a substitute for the son they'd liked to have had.

I was a college student, and since she'd had a year of college long ago, a high privilege for girls in those days before World War I, she admired me for that. My grandfather's education had ended with the seventh grade, and neither of my parents had been to college, nor had my aunt, Grandma's younger daughter.

I write these things to point out a universal yet little-understood phenomenon: God puts people in complementary relationships to meet one another's needs. I met Grandma's need to have a young college man she could admire. She met my need for a female who would listen with interest when I spoke. Such need meeting is important, especially in relationships with teen or single young adult grandchildren. For your teen or young adult grandchild, perhaps the most important "entertainment" you can give them is to listen when they talk!

◆

*Guests are like fish—they both
stink after three days,*

Benjamin Franklin once said. While there's no magic in the "three-day" limit—a happy visit may last three weeks or only three hours—there comes a time when the grandchildren need to say good-bye to Grandma's House. The duration of these visits will need to be determined upon consultation with the parents, and upon consideration of both the child's needs and your resources. A three-hour afternoon visit with your three-year-old personification of mischief may be all you can manage, but it may be all his mother needs to get her shopping done. Three days, and a five-year-old may tearfully beg to go home. A child of eight to twelve who lives half a continent away may be a joy for three weeks and beg to stay the entire three months of summer.

Some grandchildren and grandparents are temperamentally suited for each other. Others are not suited to spend long periods in each other's company. In such cases, a grandparent needs to ask the Lord for grace, while thanking him that the child has other grandparents.

Ready or not, it's up to you to make visits a pleasure your grandchildren will long remember. But more than a pleasure, a properly managed house can add immeasurably to your grandchildren's sense of security and to their maturing experience.

3

Seeing through Your Grandchild's Eyes

A sage once remarked that the elderly slow down and stoop over so that they can see things as children once again; so that they can hold the hands of children who toddle along on inexperienced feet. That bug on the sidewalk, the snail under the cabbage leaf, the robin pulling the worm from rain-moistened earth—these are the things small children and their grandparents notice.

When Christ wished to illustrate greatness he chose a child from the crowd milling about the Master Teacher and his disciples. Sitting himself among them, Jesus took that small boy on his lap. I imagine Jesus may have wiped a runny nose or tied up an errant shoelace as he spoke (see Mark 9:36-37). Jesus got down to child level, to the level of little things.

"Teacher, come see" is the cry heard again and again by the teacher of the very young. If you've taught the small ones, or if you're a grandparent, you've experienced the interruption of being called aside to view a crayon drawing, a stack of blocks just one higher than yesterday—a world record for that child—or the discovery of an exotic bug on the backside of a leaf.

◆

Children, whether toddlers or young teens,
see little things in ways adults have
forgotten how to comprehend them.

Adults may carelessly fail to appreciate and miss the opportunity to build into that grandchild much-needed concepts of competence and self worth. Children view their world as a series of small things because they lack the ability to appreciate the whole. Grandparents, on the other hand, may have to struggle to get down to a child's level.

Randy, at thirteen, has just discovered Corvettes. "Oh, wow, Grandpa! Sweet!" he explodes in ecstasy as they slide past a used car lot in Grandpa's station wagon one Saturday morning. "Stingrays—eight of 'em!"

Grandpa, a man of affairs in his late fifties, is unimpressed. He's owned cars ranging from Volkswagens to Cadillacs over forty years. An automobile is to him a convenient means of getting from point A to point B on his business rounds. *So, what's the big deal?* he's thinking.

Then it occurs to Grandpa that here's a chance to develop a relationship with Randy, and at the same time let his grandson learn a bit about the relative importance of Corvettes in the big picture of the world of transportation. So casually remarking, "Let's have a better look," he circles the block and stops under the sign reading, " 'Vette World." Moments later, Grandpa and Randy are peering under the hood of a reconditioned Corvette as Grandpa explains patiently that this particular jewel, the gee whiz of General Motors' Chevrolet line, actually has the same motor as the two-year-old station wagon they have been driving. And Randy chatters to Grandpa about acceleration rates and top speeds and streamlining— facts he dug from a borrowed auto magazine during a seventh-grade study hall.

Automobiles and insects are both "little things" in the great scheme of life. As we mature and see the larger world, both cars and bugs shrink in significance. For example, though a small child can be taught to commit to memory maps and information from a geography book almost as soon as he learns to read, the facts he may have mastered mean little to him, say child psychologists, since a child under age nine cannot grasp the topography of a world much larger than his own neighborhood. Small children must deal in little things.

But for a grown-up, looking at the little things is an art requiring cultivation. And the sooner a busy adult of middle years learns to develop this art, the sooner he or she will be able to relate meaningfully to his or her grandchildren. "A grandparent is for awe," says author Charlie Shedd. Can you enjoy with and *as* a small child such small things as the buzz of a bee on a clover blossom, the murmur of a woodland stream, the nap of the wool on a freshly shorn lamb at a county fair or petting zoo?

Shortly before I became a grandparent, I took a job as a part-time substitute teacher to bridge the gap between a career as an instructor in a college that closed its doors and a new career as a writer. My experience had been as a secondary teacher, so I signed up for that department. Though I had kids of my own—by then teens and young adults—and could recall taking them on my knee when they were small to read to them or dry their tears, the idea of my taking charge of two or three dozen elf-sized humanoids, each with his peculiar needs, unnerved me.

Then one morning early the phone rang. It was the sub caller for an elementary school, and she was desperate. A fourth-grade teacher had suddenly been taken ill. Ruefully I agreed to take her place.

I soon learned that fourth graders—nine-year-olds—are peaches and cream. So are third, second, and first graders. Kindergarteners, too. Few things lift my day more than half a dozen small ones (usually girls!) jumping up and down outside the classroom window at a quarter to eight screaming, "Hey, we've got a *MAN* for a teacher today!"

But then comes the small stuff—a day filled with the little things of life. An uncoordinated boy who has to have his boots pulled on and his coat zipped every recess. Chairs so low that if you join the reading circle you must park your legs off to the side. Endless crayon pictures of houses with chimneys perpendicular to the pitch of the roof—you admire the artwork and patiently show the second grader that chimneys go straight up and down. Then there's the gerbil that needs to be fed and, yes, petted by the children and admired by you—all the while you're wishing the cage had a padlock and only you had a key!

◆

Children are little, and their concerns and complaints are little in adult eyes, so you and I must become little in order to truly appreciate them.

In my second-grade classroom, an adopted Chinese girl with a Polish name, Maria Shozenski, was hurt because the boy behind her (also Polish!) called her a "squint-eyed Chink." I mended her spirits by telling her that "God must love Chinese, because he made more of them than any other people." Two years later Maria showed up in a fourth-grade class where I was the substitute, and she remembered me and told me, "Mother says you're right; there *are* more Chinese than any other people." I've got a friend for life!

The kenosis passage, Philippians 2:5-8, best expresses the attitude that Christian grandparents must assume if they are to meet the needs of their grandchildren. Christ "made himself of no reputation," the King James Bible says. This is a translation of a single Greek verb, *kenoo*, "to empty." He "emptied himself" is a marginal reference in my Bible. J.B. Phillips translates this "stripped himself of all privilege." This is precisely what Jesus was illustrating when he picked up the child in Mark 9:36-37. Our willingness to empty ourselves of adult privilege, to become nothing, that we may experience the little things with our grandchildren is the measure of our ability to communicate with our grandchildren.

It grieves me to see an adult caricature a child. I recall an elderly woman who had no children of her own who was a guest in our home for a while when I was a teenager. She had little use for children (my parents then had five). When she wanted to speak to a small child she'd talk baby talk, demeaning the child's attempts to express himself. But mere imitation is mockery, and this is sensed by the child for the fraud that it is. Rather, to know a child you must *be* a child.

On the practical level, the little things are bridges to our rapport with our grandchildren, if we will but put ourselves on the child's plane. Grasping life a piece at a time is the way each of us had to learn life's great lessons so long ago, and this is how our Randys and Katys are even now learning them.

Our grandchildren live in imperfect homes, reared by imperfect parents—our sons or daughters who are married to our sons-in-law or daughters-in-law, all of them imperfect. Although we made mistakes raising our grandchildren's parents, the good news is that godly grandparents who walk with the Lord can expect the Lord to use them to fill in gaps where, because of our own immaturity when our children (now parents) were growing up, we let them down.

In the rush of the young-or-middle-aged adult world, little things tend to go by the board. That's partly because adults are so busy assembling the little things to make a complete picture that we lose sight of the pieces. While daddies are working for a promotion, building a business, repairing the house, grandfathers are needed to fix Junior's bicycle, wipe little Susie's nose, or even help an older grandson change a fuel pump.

Mothers, for instance, don't like to clean fish; some will refuse to do so. So eight-year-old Ernie shows up at dinnertime with an assortment of aquatic denizens he's pulled on baited hook from the creek under the highway bridge behind your subdivision: three shiners, a sunfish, two perch, and a catfish. "Leave the fish in the shed and wash up," Mother calls, her irritation betraying her dread of helping Ernie clean them. "I don't know what you brought those fish home for, anyway. Your grandmother's freezer is full of them, and she gives us all we want. Besides, I'm sure that stream is polluted."

Dinner over, Ernie turns to the TV, and Dad goes out to wax the car. He sets the bucket of fish on the shady side of the yard building, and while he's at work, Bowser has *his* supper—Ernie's catch of the day!

But a week later, Ernie's parents, having been remorseful at being so careless with Ernie's fish, leave him with Grandma overnight. Her village home is near a lake with a lagoon which runs behind her street. As the sun sets over the lake, Ernie and Grandma are casting their lines where the blue gills and perch are the hungriest.

From this experience, young Ernie learns an important lesson about the food chain (fish eat worms; people and dogs eat fish). More importantly, he learns that his fish, so important to him because he's caught them himself, are important to a person very special in his life— Grandma. Grandma helps Ernie bait his hook and shows him how to disengage a barb from a fish's mouth. She makes an assembly line process of cleaning the fish she and he have caught together by spreading cutting boards and newspapers on her back-porch table where heads, fins, scales, and innards can be removed by Grandma, who has learned not to be squeamish, and by Ernie, who has not yet learned squeamishness.

The next day when Mother picks Ernie up at Grandma's house, Ernie proudly presents her a frozen package labeled, "Ernie's fish"—to which Grandma has added several she caught herself. Ernie's shining eyes tell the story: He is a very important person to Grandma, for Grandma accepted his fish as valuable, and she even helped him clean them as he helped with hers, bolstering his self worth even more. And his parents, who had been planning on broiled salmon (at $6.89 a pound!) for dinner, gamely help Ernie eat them and call them delicious.

"Little things mean a lot" is a lyric of a song on the radio forty or so years ago. Little things mean a lot to the little people in our lives, for to them, these are the stuff life is made of—a young teen's interest in an auto, a small boy's fish. I wonder what were the memories of the boy who saw his little lunch of five biscuit-sized loaves and two tiny fish used to feed the throng by

Galilee? Isn't it possible that this unnamed lad was later one of the great men of the book of Acts who tramped across Europe to plant churches with the apostle Paul, motivated by the multiplication of his work at the word of the Master?

A nickel is a little piece of change, but how well I remember greedily clutching mine when Grandma placed it in my greasy palm and pointed me toward where Grandpa was already selecting blue and red helium-filled balloons from a vendor at the county fairgrounds. How I gripped that coin, sure that if I dropped it in the milling throng my opportunity for this new (to me!) marvel, a lighter-than-air balloon, would be gone forever. Had not Grandpa, an important sheriff who got free admission by simply flashing his silver badge, warned me that pickpockets lurked behind every tent?

We jounced across the hills toward home, brother George and I, in the back of Grandpa's old panel truck, our balloons secured by their strings to our wrists. That night Mother untied the strings, and our balloons soared wonderfully to the ceiling. I don't recall another thing about that trip to the fair, but I do recall the generosity of my grandparents who drove with us to what seemed to me then like the outer edge of the world to return with a treasure more delightful than Marco Polo could have discovered in old Cathay—a helium-filled balloon.

How deep my disappointment to find our balloons on the floor next morning, their buoyancy gone, lifeless, half limp, dead things that had surely cheated Grandma out of two nickels!

It is Grandma's thoughtfulness that lives on in my memory, though. Creatures of our appetites that my brother and I were, we'd have readily spent as many nickels as we could bribe our grandparents out of on cotton candy, ice cream, strawberry sodas, or deep-fried elephant ears. But Grandma knew that a five-cent helium balloon (uninflated ones were two for a penny), a little thing to her, would delight us long after the ice cream had dripped all over our home-made overalls and the spun sugar had been smeared all across our cheeks.

◆

If you would lift your grandchild as Christ
lifted a child, you must see small things
as they are seen through small eyes.

Even as the life of those gas-filled balloons was brief, childhood is brief in adult terms. Think back to when you passed a minor milestone in your life, say seven or eight years ago. Perhaps you bought the car you're now driving, purchased a piece of furniture, or a nice pair of leather-lined dress shoes (mine last fifteen years!). Think of your grandchild who was born about then, or since. You are fifty, or perhaps seventy or eighty. But that grandchild, like yourself, is exactly one lifetime old. And you must fit yourself into that tiny life, a span of time so short it seems just the other day, while that grandchild is still little enough for you to make meaningful, important marks on him.

4

The Extended Family: Yesterday and Today

When my sister traced our family tree's branches back to its varied roots, she found a tangle of extended families, including several intermarriages, most of which sprang since the Revolutionary War from a plot of rural Central Maine soil with a radius of not more than a dozen miles from our family home. Our farmstead, where five generations of Wiggins lived for a century, was typical of our community. Uncle Oscar (or Cousin Oscar, depending on which side of our family you figured the relationship), for instance, spent most of his 102 years (1882-1984) in the house where he was born, less than a mile from our place. His house, in fact, had been built three quarters of a century before his birth by Oscar's great-grandfather when our country lane was still a pack-horse trail and the land covered with virgin pine.

The extended family I knew as a child included paternal grandparents, who lived in the house with us—the house built by my grandfather, where my father spent his entire life and where both his parents died in the bedroom they shared for half a century. It included also my maternal grandparents, just two miles away in a home shared with my great-grandmother and an unmarried aunt. A mile away lived my grandmother's brother and wife in a house built by Grandma's father; and three miles farther on dwelt another aunt and uncle and a house full of cousins.

My wife's family came from the rural South, and after a few years in suburban St. Louis they moved to the upper Midwest's industrial belt to find employment. Their move was a family affair: the grandparents came along as did brothers, sisters, and cousins, like the Okies' exodus to California in *The Grapes of Wrath*. Just before our marriage, I became the last recipient of my wife's grandmother's lecture on how to treat a wife, a family tradition which I have since learned began before I was born. So many relatives from nearby communities were on our wedding-guest list that we had to rent a church building in a neighboring village—her family's church would not hold the crowd!

Months after we were married, my wife and I attended a Polish wedding in Detroit's inner city, where we learned of another type of extended family. Both bride and groom were descended from immigrants from Eastern Europe, and tables were spread in a church basement for a Polish feast for perhaps 200 guests, many of them family members from the same city neighborhood.

Whittier's biographical poem, "Snowbound," paints a picture of a pre-Civil War extended family of several generations, sheltered under one roof. "Shut in from all the world without, We sat the clean-winged hearth about," he wrote. Grandparents, parents, and unmarried aunts, with the children, filled that family circle in the firelight in that New England homestead.

◆

The extended family, as Whittier pictured it, has dispersed across America in several stages.

First, the industrialization of America in the three quarters of a century between the Civil War and World War II has taken Americans from the farm. This has usually meant that grandparents no longer live in the same house with children and grandchildren or even in near proximity. Too, money from industrial jobs, as well as massive federal subsidies of housing since the war, has made it possible for millions of young American couples to live in their own houses—the bungalows and duplexes of the forties and fifties, the split-levels of the sixties and seventies, and presently homes of four bedrooms and two baths with two-stall garages in burgeoning subdivisions, almost palatial by standards prevalent when today's grandparents were children.

Satellite clusters of houses have sprung up outside cities beyond the suburbs along expressway systems built since the war, giving our language a new word:

exurbia. Many families that once enjoyed the support of their extended families in ethnic neighborhoods, such as the Polish districts of Detroit and Chicago or Irish neighborhoods in Boston, have been scattered to the cities' perimeter and beyond. American families now move once in five years, on average, seeking more modern housing or because of job changes. Young couples with children move more often than this; older couples less often.

Too, World War II brought with it increased employment for women. This trend has continued for the half century since the war, as automatic appliances have freed both rural and city housewives from household drudgery, and packaged foods and cheap restaurants have released many women from doing what their grandmothers called "fixin' a meal." The first wave of mothers to take jobs away from home (during the war years, 1941-1945) are now grandmothers and great-grandmothers. Like their daughters, many are reluctant to rebuild an extended family circle; many, in fact, do not even understand the concept.

The alienation of the extended family has for many been made complete by the move of older couples into retirement communities, often hundreds of miles from the kids and grandkids.

Florida, Arizona, and parts of California have seen droves of elderly seeking to escape the city for the sun, though upper New England and many pockets in the rural South have large settlements of retirees also.

Government grants underwriting nursing home construction, along with Medicaid and Social Security, have, since the late sixties, made it possible for millions of elderly—the older grandparents and great-grandparents—to spend their final years in nursing homes. Even the poorest elderly person can often get nursing home care by selling off his or her assets, spending the money, then declaring himself indigent in order to qualify for Medicaid funding. Younger grandmothers, entering the work force as soon as their children leave the nest at eighteen, often simply will not later forgo a weekly paycheck to nurse Great-grandma at home.

But the picture is not as bleak as it may seem. *Reader's Digest*'s roving editor Fred Barnes reports (July '92) that though TV typically portrays as normal the lives of bar-hopping singles and wife-swapping marrieds, giving "little" and "scornful" attention to "families who hold traditional values," a major *Reader's Digest* poll in early 1992 found that "the old virtues (of families with children) are quietly exalted in the suburbs and rural areas and urban residential neighborhoods where families live." Notes Barnes, "That's where traditional values, conservatism, and religion prosper."

Barnes found, in fact, that though media reports tout the statistic that only 26 percent of homes are traditional, with a mother, father, and children under eighteen, these homes actually make up 41 percent of the population. Add to this figure the millions of households where there are no children because the couples are newlyweds, and the couples who are grandparents whose children have married, and in fact traditional American homes do still make up a solid majority.

Realistically, American families are not going to return to living on farms and in small villages in great numbers. The back-to-the-land movement, 1970-1990, leveled off with the recession of the 1990s. Indeed, many back-to-landers were themselves grandparents buying worked-out small farms for retirement homes. But in the 1990s, the grain-belt states, such as Iowa and South Dakota, are rapidly losing young families who've moved to the cities for jobs, leaving grandparents far from the grandchildren. Iowa, for example, had twice the national average of elderly over age eighty-five because of this trend, reports Elliott Carlson in the June 1992 *AARP Bulletin.*

◆

Many grandparents are now more "able to afford"
living in their own homes than in the past.

Cynthia Taeuber, chief of the age and sex statistics branch of the U.S. Census Bureau, reported this to *Bulletin* writer Carlson. This is having the double-edged effect of more grandparents living alone longer than in the past, keeping them from moving in with their children and grandchildren. On the other hand, this gives enough financial security so that most never need to live in a nursing home, a positive effect, since grandparents living in their own homes are much more accessible to grandchildren than those who are institutionalized. And, despite the growth in the nursing-home industry in the last quarter century, only one fourth of grandparents over eighty-five live in institutions, and a far lesser number of those age sixty-five to eighty-five.

It is possible in most cases to keep even an invalid elderly grandparent at home without major financial or physical burdens on other family members. Some seven million American households currently have grandparents living with an adult son or daughter because they need aid in doing household chores, or because they are no longer able to attend to all of their personal bodily needs, says Horace B. Deets, executive director of the American Association of Retired Persons *(Bulletin,* June '92). This is beneficial to holding a family together, certainly. But how unlike the pattern typical of yesteryear, when on the farm, grandparents were often living with adult children when they were still able to take an active part in household duties and grandchildren were still at home.

I can still envision my paternal grandmother, a tall, rugged woman, though nearly half a century older than my pixie-sized mother, as the two of them canned beans or tomatoes for the winter larder. Though nearly eighty, she would without hesitation wrestle a heavy, fully loaded pressure canner from the stove across the kitchen to the sink to cool it off. Mother, who preferred to unload the canner a quart at a time where it sat, eventually became Grandma's caregiver in the home where both women spent their married lives after Grandma, past ninety, was confined to a wheelchair.

In a move to cut Medicare costs, Michigan and several other states have started a Home Health Services program, which a Michigan Department of Social Services spokesperson says is "much less expensive" for the taxpayer than nursing-home confinement. For instance, the John Hancock Mutual Life Insurance company reports (1992) that elderly institutional care in the upper Midwest costs an average of $35,000 per patient. The Home Health Services program, however, provides a daughter or daughter-in-law with needed cash for extra expenses, such as hiring a part-time caregiver.

◆

Many existing extended families can be preserved, and still others reunited, if the members will consider each other's needs before their own.

God's will for most of us is to live in a family (see Ps. 68:6). Families are for loving, and sharing, and burden-bearing (see John 13:34-35). Despite the forces which tear families apart, the late twentieth century is filled with opportunities for family unity as never before.

The idea of actively taking moves to keep or draw an extended family together is so opposite the habitual thinking of many American Christians that these concepts may seem strange. Part of the problem, I believe, is that as creatures of extremes, we have placed an overemphasis on Bible passages telling us, like Sherwin Williams paint, to spread out across the earth. For example, the Bible teaches that a man should "leave his father and mother" as he is "joined unto his wife" (Gen. 2:24; Eph. 5:32). The Lord called Abraham to leave his father's house in Chaldea and journey to Canaan where his family would be made a great nation. Abraham, however, passed several years in Syria along the way, and his delay is often used (correctly) to illustrate how Christians may get sidetracked into easy paths when God calls them to leave their families to go to a distant land (see Gen. 11:31; Luke 9:57-60).

There is, however, no doctrine in the Word of God requiring that one abandon his family. Two principles here require brief consideration:

First, when the children are growing up, parents and grandparents should not live in the same household, ordinarily. A man is to "leave his father and mother": not abandon them, but leave the house. No wife should be required to live in her mother-in-law's shadow. Disagreements and bickering on matters such as child discipline can leave children confused.

Some, by no means all, families are called of God to move to remote corners of the earth for the purpose of the ministry of the gospel. In the case of my own family, after three years in a pastorate, shortly before my father's death at age fifty-one the Lord opened the door to a teaching position and further education in Indiana, a thousand miles from my parents' home in Maine. Though the tie-breaking was difficult, I, my wife, and two children made the move to a city where one of my brothers already lived. A year later, Mother and her three children still at home followed. Now my kids had Grandma living just around the block, and their Michigan grandparents were able to visit often.

We have moved several times since to follow the Lord in varied Christian ministries: to Michigan, North Carolina, back to Maine, and finally to settle again in Michigan, near the children's maternal grandmother and an easy drive from their other grandmother in Indiana.

The Lord leads, and he sometimes intervenes in our "best-laid plans." But as we build our homes—whether a retirement home or a home for still-at-home children—plan with keeping the extended family together in mind. And when Great-grandma or Great-grandpa can no longer care for themselves, we who are younger grandparents, whose own children have left, married, and left us with empty rooms, should give serious thought to taking them in.

U.S. Census Bureau official Cynthia Taeuber says the so-called "sandwich generation" theory touted in the press, that mothers are frequently trapped into tending their own parents as soon as, or right after, their own children leave and marry "is a bogus issue." Rather, says Ms. Taeuber, most folks who give care to homebound great-grandparents have seen all their children leave years earlier, and they are grandparents themselves in many cases. Resistance to home care, she says, "isn't so much the increasing numbers of elderly people as the fact that adult daughters," themselves often grandmothers, have taken jobs after their kids were grown and don't wish to give them up.

◆

*Opportunities often exist for
surrogate grandparenting, if we but
open our eyes and hearts to them.*

For example, during our five years living in coastal New England, with our four children ages 2 through 14, 7 through 19 when we left, I owned a rototiller, but I had no garden plot. An elderly widow from our church lived nearby, and she had a large back yard of rich soil but only a small garden and no tiller. I arranged with her to allow me to till up her yard, where we both could garden with the help of my youngsters.

This lady soon became "Grammy Jackson" to my kids, though she had some two dozen grandchildren of her own. Adding my four to her multitude of grandkids did not crowd her schedule, and my children learned to appreciate and love a person of age and wisdom, though both their grandmothers were a thousand miles away in the Midwest.

Offering yourself as a surrogate grandparent must be done quietly, with tact, but with an open heart and home. It may begin with giving a neighbor's kids a ride to Sunday school, offering them milk and cookies, or by Grandpa fixing a swing set for the family next door.

All too easily we fret, "I don't mind spending money or time on my *own* grandkids." We may forget that when we selflessly give of our resources to build spiritual values into the lives of other's children, we lay up treasures in heaven—real jewels—and make the world a better place for our own grandchildren's generation, to boot (see Mal. 3:17; Matt. 6:19-21; 19:13-15)!

Young families with children in your church, if they are isolated from their children's grandparents, may appreciate being included in a holiday back-yard cookout. Or you might relieve the harried mother of a newborn by taking the older children to the zoo, accepting no pay. Churches near Christian colleges, for instance, often have married students in their congregations with children in need of grandparenting. The opportunities to grandparent the children of families in your church, isolated by miles or other circumstances from their own senior members, are as legion as with your own grandchildren—and as big as your heart!

5

Grandfather's Mountain

Walton's Mountain is where all the good things happen, where the family always sticks together, where everything always turns out right, according to the old TV serial. "Give me this mountain" as a reward for my service to God's people, said old Caleb (Josh. 14:12). Caleb's Mount Hebron became the possession of his heirs in perpetuity.

Many grandfathers can and should establish a family homestead, a "Mountain" where their children can bring the grandchildren. Too many of today's youngsters are robbed of the privilege of going to Grandma's House because their grandparents have retired to Florida or Arizona, leaving the grandchildren with no Mountain as a refuge.

In readying Grandfather's Mountain (or Grandmother's Mountain) for the enjoyment and nurture of grandchildren, an accessible location is much more important than spacious accommodations. I have visited numerous such Mountains over the years, for grandparents who are hospitable toward their grandchildren tend to be big-hearted men and women who open their homes to others, also. One such Mountain is a small house on the dead end of an older residential street in the midst of a bustling city. A small, undeveloped field, the property of an industrial plant the next street over, lay just outside the grandfather's back door. So, with the permission of the plant's manager, this grandpa managed a large garden there over many years, and he kept the rest of the area mowed so that his grandchildren, who visited from their homes on the city's outskirts, could romp and play.

Some grandfathers, because of their lifestyles, have built up over their younger years these family Mountains, which in future years can be used to build family relationships. Others, when they reach their mid-to-late forties, must plan carefully lest this greatest blessing of their golden years, the fellowship of their grandchildren, slip from them. In the case of the grandfather on the dead-end street, he had reared four children in this home. As he reached retirement, with time on his hands, he took up gardening. The empty lot was available, and the other circumstances of life, such as having grandchildren nearby, just seemed naturally to fall into place.

Jim and Shirley Franks raised ten children, four of them adopted Korean orphans, in a house at a busy in-town intersection. We had "all the noise and everything, and I really craved to get away from it," remembers Grandpa Franks. So the Franks bought ten wooded acres running back to a muddy lake just outside the small

Midwest city where they'd raised their own children. "I did this specifically for my grandkids" (there are twenty-three of them now, newborn to young adult), says Jim. "The grandkids can row a boat, swim, help in the garden, run—do whatever they want out there." You can certainly tell this gives him pleasure.

Over the years, Jim and Shirley have added several wings to what was once a modest ranch-style house, all aimed at accommodating grandchildren who've come from as far as Japan and Africa, or who live only minutes away. Jim is an expert horticulturalist who's served with missionary relief organizations for forty years, and his garden and small orchard give little ones the opportunity for satisfying hands-on experiences under Grandpa's supervision.

Not all retirement homes turn out as happily as the Franks', however. For instance, Christian grandparents Joe and Alice Hayden (names and certain details have been changed), responded to the old adage that "you can take a boy out of the country, but you can't take the country out of the boy." Joe took early retirement from his city job, and he bought a farm in Minnesota near where he'd grown up, and where Joe and Alice and their three boys had vacationed on occasion. Their retirement home, however, was hundreds of miles from the children and eight grandchildren, all of whom had settled near the city where they'd been raised.

Joe reasoned that he'd get to see his grandchildren on the occasions when their parents vacationed in Minnesota. Perhaps he could augment this by sending the grandkids an occasional bus ticket to their backwoods community. But the children and grandchildren usually preferred vacations at Disney World or the beach to the Minnesota forest. Even on holidays, it was Grandpa and Grandma who were forced to make an all-day drive to see their family.

So Joe Hayden poured his savings and energy into building up a rundown farm. The sheep and beef cattle he herded on woodland pastures barely paid for themselves, but Joe was enjoying fixing fences, repairing the barn and house, and tending his livestock. A collie, which became his daily companion, rode beside him in the jeep as Joe checked on cattle in the back pastures.

But in a dozen years, Joe's health failed. He was forced to sell the farm. Oh, he might merely have auctioned off the cattle and machinery and stayed put. But Alice missed the grandchildren. To tell the truth, now that health constraints had forced him to slow down, Joe longed for his family also.

They moved back to their old neighborhood. They found a house with a spacious lot, and Joe, still a farmer at heart, planted fruit trees and a large garden. The Haydens tried to take up where they'd left off. But they couldn't. The grandchildren, all toddlers and preschoolers when their grandparents had moved to Minnesota, were now teens.

Joe and Alice now entertain their three families from time to time. Sometimes they have all-adult parties. But on occasion, one or more of the grandchildren will accompany their parents to Grandpa and Grandma's house, then slip away to their cars as soon as they are done eating to spend time with their teen friends.

"A man's heart plans his course, but the Lord directs his steps," is the advice of Solomon, who had a very large family indeed (Prov. 16:9, paraphrased). As we grow older, many of us see retirement as a chance to work out unfulfilled longings. Life under Florida palms, fishing, golfing, touring—or for some, a return to childhood roots, perhaps to farm. Any of these retirement pursuits are fine in themselves, but as we "plan our course" it's all too easy to take self-directed "steps," rather than heeding the Lord's direction. If farming, for example, is what you desire, can you find a farm near enough so that you can enjoy your Herefords and your grandchildren, too? Might it not be possible to satisfy your craving for Florida sunshine by spending a few weeks there in a camping trailer in the dead of winter, then returning to Grandfather's Mountain for the rest of the year?

Children and grandchildren are spoken of in the Bible as a "reward" of the righteous, as the "crown" of the elderly (see Ps. 127:3-5; 128:6; Prov. 17:6). We too easily blame the young for their wayward ways, yet often we're so far away we can't nurture them, aiding the values we cherish to be carried out in our grandchildren.

Christian grandparents who would help turn the tide of rootless youth can build a Mountain where their own grandchildren can retreat for shelter. But don't expect every one of your grandchildren to realize they *need* this shelter from the storms of life. *You* provide it; invite them often while they're still small, and they'll find their way there when they're in their teens or are young marrieds with children of their own, bringing blessing to the fourth generation (see Prov. 22:6).

Here are some suggestions for your own Mountain building:

◆

*Don't tie up a lot of money
in a large or expensive house.*

Pay off your mortgage in fifteen years or so. Then if in late middle age you have an urge to relocate, you can do so with grandchildren in mind and with the ability to pay cash for the new home. This will leave you with resources to renovate with an eye to entertaining the family.

◆

*Consider
staying put.*

Most grandpas today don't own country homes, of course, and perhaps only a few can hope to own such a place when they retire. But a small house on a large lot in a quiet, older neighborhood may be exactly what you need. Add a deck where you can have a barbecue. Enclose a porch, then add a studio couch where a grandchild can sleep. Install a swing set and a sandbox in the back yard. A basketball hoop next to a paved drive will keep pre-teen and teen boys busy for hours. Lay in a supply of lawn games such as badminton, volleyball, croquet, and horseshoes.

Most any home in an urban or suburban neighborhood can be adjusted, at modest expense, to accommodate grandkids. Consider turning the garage into a family room or extra bedroom if you don't have room to expand, or can't afford to add a wing. The garage door framing can be left in place in case a subsequent owner wishes to return it to garage use. Though making an unattached garage into living quarters may violate zoning codes, such buildings nevertheless make great places to set up ping pong or pool tables, and insulation and a gas or kerosene heater can make them usable even in cold weather. If codes permit, a hutch of rabbits or even a small coop of chickens will give the small ones endless fascination. And perhaps you might run an underground electrical cable and cold water line to the back fence, so that family members with camping trailers can park there on occasion.

◆

Purchase a large,
newer mobile home

in a well-kept trailer park which has an ample recreation and banquet hall that can be rented for a modest fee. If a swimming pool and game courts are adjacent, all the better. Grandparents who are the parents of seven married children living in the Midwest found such accommodations when their home proved inadequate to entertain their more than two dozen grandkids. Their mobile home's extra bedroom and bath will accommodate one of their out-of-town families for a short stay, or two or more grandchildren for as long as the grandparents care to keep them. But the recreation hall, rented for a holiday, birthday, or a grandchild's graduation party, rings with the merry laughter of the grandchildren several times a year, and in summer the small ones splash in the adjacent pool as the older family members eat potluck style inside.

◆

*Purchase a
country home,*

if that is your urge and you can afford to do so. A diligent search may turn up a livable old farmhouse with a few acres just outside the city where you now live. Such arrangements are far more versatile than a house in a subdivision, though it's easy to spend a bundle on fixing up such a place if you are the kind of person who must have everything flawlessly decorated. Here's where a grandfather handy with tools can double his family's benefits. Financially, the family gains as he does his own repairs and remodeling. And he builds bonds with grandchildren as he teaches them self-sufficient skills while they work with him in building a rabbit hutch or painting the porch.

*Grandfather's Mountain need
not be a principal residence,*

if it is centrally located and accessible to the grandchildren. A retired couple in Maine, both who worked at
a Christian summer children's camp, parked their camping trailer on a lakefront cottage lot near the camp. Soon
they built a cottage shell around the camper, thus adding
a living room, bedrooms, and a screened porch—all of
which are filled with grandchildren much of the summer.
These grandparents, giving of themselves in their retirement years to help the children of others, found themselves, in turn, helping their own grandchildren. And, as
with the Franks, they set an example of selfless service
their children and grandchildren could follow.

*Grandfather's Mountain
should include a workshop,*

if possible. Pre-teen and teen boys, especially, are attracted to productive, creative adult activity. The visits I
remember best to my grandfather's house or to the
homes of friends' grandfathers have involved creative
male activity (though girls often love it, too!).

I remember standing sneaker-top deep in the pine
shavings of Grandpa Fuller's woodworking shop or

watching Uncle Raymond (now a great-grandfather) roll a log into the blade of his sawmill, a "toy" he'd bought at retirement. At family reunions, myself, my brothers, and cousins would explore Great-uncle Willie's marvelous wood-and-mechanical shop until we were rebuked by fearful parents. A grandfather of my acquaintance has turned his two-car garage into a auto-service shop popular with his grandsons. Still another grandfather has set up a fish-fly tying bench in a small tool shed behind his house, where grandsons and grand-nephews sometimes congregate to learn his art.

One of my earliest memories was visiting with my father what I have since learned was probably the last blacksmith shop in our state. Elderly John Harding, soot-covered, in leather apron, heated cherry red in his forge the iron bolts Daddy had brought. He pounded them into angles on his anvil, then quenched them in a barrel of water.

A child has no appreciation for nostalgia. So I can say assuredly that my appreciation then of the old blacksmith's work was in having the creativity born in me from God drawn out by this unusual (to me) creative activity. As magnetic iron attracts iron, so the soul of a child, created to create, is attracted by creativity (see Gen. 1:27).

The possibilities for workshops are endless, from hobbies to serious adult employment. It strengthens a growing youth's grasp on reality and fires his creativity, I believe, to see a grandfather at productive activity as well as at play.

◆

*Some grandfathers cannot build
a Mountain for their grandchildren,*

of course. They may be limited by financial constraints, or by life in an apartment or condo, from which they cannot afford to move. Or a divorce may have disjointed the family, leaving not only the family's resources limited, but ties with children's families badly strained. Partial solutions in such cases can be found by renting facilities at public parks for weekend outings. Many communities have municipally owned banquet rooms or halls; or the local VFW or other civic organization may have rooms available for a modest fee. Churches can and should help, as well, by permitting families of limited means to use the church's fellowship hall and kitchen (see Acts 2:44-45).

My own experience with Grandfather's Mountain takes a chapter right out of *The Waltons.* In fact, there were several Mountains in my childhood which served as refuges and places where I could enjoy adult companionship and mature words of wisdom. My mother's parents' New England country inn, already more than a century old at my birth, pops up in several places in this book, so I'll not describe it here, except to say that I would sometimes purposely miss the school bus, then enjoy a long talk with my grandmother as an interlude in a three-mile walk home. Mother's uncle, an elderly widower who was a trapper, lived a mile farther along our graveled road. Since his eyes were weak and he could not drive, I could usually find Uncle Oscar reading with a magnifying glass beside his stove, ready to regale my young imagination with tales of shooting a bobcat or trapping a bear. My dad's elder sister, a schoolteacher not blessed with children of her own, lived with her husband in a Cape Cod house with its long ell attached to a barn farther up the hill. Aunt Gladys, who was also a pastry cook at a summer resort, made the best raspberry pie a boy ever tasted from berries which grew half wild behind their horse stable. Her pies more than once enticed me to fill a lard pail with berries without pay, braving the briars and the hornets which lurked among them to gather my reward.

But the Mountain I remember best is the rambling, Victorian farmhouse built by Grandpa Wiggin in 1899-1900. He came with his parents in 1869 to what for a century was our family's homestead, where they lived in a Cape Cod farmhouse built some thirty years earlier. Shortly after Grandpa built the house where I and my father were both born and grew up, the old Cape burned, though its circa 1840 barn stood until I grew into adulthood.

Grandpa built his house rather large for the family of three he raised there, and the upstairs was not fully finished until his children were adults. But his two sons found room there for upstairs apartments, where their oldest children were born, and a fourth generation—my own first two—lived there, also, for a time.

The quarter-section, Maine hillside farm of 160 acres, more or less, was explored nook and cranny by me over the years. I learned every square inch of the house, barn, and horse stable—bereft of horses and converted into a machine shop by my father. Probably to a greater extent than my dad, who as the youngest son of older parents grew up without grandparents, on that Mountain I learned to appreciate the continuity of life, coupled with the practicality of small things. I learned, for example, to treasure the hours of sultry August afternoons, when on the screened back porch next to a grove of pines I would snap beans by the bushel for Mother's canner, or cut up apples for pies and sauce. And, after winter hours on Saturday helping Grandpa split and stack stovewood, I learned to listen, or ply him with questions, as he talked beside the wood-fired kitchen range of events long ago in terms a small boy could relate to, sometimes punctuating his discourse with words of wisdom from experience or the Proverbs of the Bible.

Grand*fathers* should take the lead in preparing a place where the grandkids can visit, a Mountain of shelter from the storms of growing up. Too often, the initiative is left to Grandma, who must work around Grandpa's TV ballgames, his golf outings, hunting and fishing trips, or his just not wanting to be bothered by children. But grandfathers have a responsibility, I believe, not only to make provision for grandchildren, but to encourage grandmas to invite them over, and to make themselves available for loving interaction with the grandkids. Instead of going fishing alone, take your grandchild with you.

One teen girl, deeply hurt by her parents' divorce, had determined never to date boys or marry. But after spending a few days with her loving, Christian grandparents, seeing them not only interact with love toward each other but observing that they kept romance alive—even to smooching on the back-porch swing in the moon-light—she had a complete reversal in her attitude.

God gives grandparents to grandkids largely, I believe, because parents are imperfect. We grandparents can be there to fill the gaps in our children's attention toward their own children by furnishing the grandchildren with mature role models, by lending them our sympathetic adult ears to listen when their parents are preoccupied with other pursuits, and by letting them know that they are important to adults who love them, thus giving them confidence to step forward into maturity. Each grand-father should seek to erect his own Mountain where these ends may be carried out.

6

When Grandmas and Grandpas Were Old

Recently I passed an old man on a bicycle. It was a battered, fat-tired velocipede of the kind popular when I was a kid. The fellow wore a crumpled felt hat and ragged pants tied at the cuffs with rubber bands, which made all the more conspicuous his unshined brown dress shoes, the uppers cracked, soles peeling off. A battered lunch box was wired to his handlebars.

Recently I passed an old man on a bicycle. His shock of snow-white hair was sharply accented by a cranberry jogging suit. Lime-green tennis shoes adorned the feet which spun the pedals of his new, fifteen-speed tourer as he breezed along with a red Irish setter loping behind.

Time was, grandparents on bikes looked as queer as the poor fellow in the first paragraph. Though my grandfather once said he could ride a bicycle, I'd never seen him on one, and I'm sure I'd have laughed had he tried mine. Grandparents in those days were supposed to be staid, dignified, sensible.

I asked Shirley Franks, a grandmother whose memories reach back almost to the Victorian era, if she recalled when grandmas were old. "Grandmas wore navy blue, then," she laughed, patting her white polyester slacks, "navy blue and polka dots for variety. At least they had more choices than the men!"

This matriarch of some two dozen grandchildren ranging from newborn to young adult told of sitting on her own grandmother's lap. "I pulled the skin on the back of Grandma's hand. It was loose," she said, "like mine, today." She tugged a loose fold on the back of her own hand. "'Grandma, you're *old*,' I said," she merrily recalled. "Grandmas today look for the misses department when we buy our clothes!"

This observation points up some very subtle changes in our culture that we've pretty much adjusted to without understanding what's happened. Some of these changes have been for the good, and others are a part of a dangerous social subculture. If we as grandparents are to affect following generations for the good, we need to understand the influences which have changed—not just our choices in clothing but our total lifestyles—and adjust our thinking to embrace the good, resist the bad, and be discriminating whichever we do.

First, there's a rush toward modernity that's been a part of the industrialized Western World since well back in the nineteenth century but which accelerated after World War II. For example, synthetic fabrics and color-fast dyes led to a rampage of avant-garde clothing experiments in the 1950s and 1960s. Then came the move toward natural and organic products of the late 60s and 70s. But the 80s and 90s have brought a mellowing and blending of these trends, and today's clothing, usually of blended or chemically processed fabrics, is neither a reflection of the slick fifties nor the saggy seventies, but a happy mixture of the best of both.

The millenia-old beliefs that the old should advise the young, and that the elderly should let their bodies age, concentrating sensibly on improving their souls and minds, had been reversed in a generation. Physical culture is the fad of our age. Breast implants, tummy-tuck operations, wrinkle removal by surgery, daily regimens of weight lifting, biking, and jogging have become the rage. Many grandfathers wile away their evenings watching well-muscled youths chase an inflated pigskin across a field of astroturf. Not to be outdone, the grannies spend hours imitating the antics of acrobatic aerobics instructors.

Is there a balance? I think so.

First, we grandparents must firmly retake the lead, if not of society as a whole, at least of our own families. This is not as drastic a step as it may seem, for the pendulum has begun to swing the other way, and maturity is coming into fashion again. White-haired Barbara Bush, with her throng of grandchildren, has been accepted as a spokesperson by many American women. Andy Griffith and Raymond Burr have been reworked as sagacious, silver-locked Ben Matlock and bearded, mature Perry Mason. In Christian circles, Billy Graham, past threescore and ten, is still the most admired man in

America, and Jack Wyrtzen, past eighty, is still loved as a leader of youth and older folks alike. Congress has responded to the ambitions of millions of older folks to continue working past seventy without the loss of Social Security.

For most of us, however, the point where the tire touches the asphalt is facing our personal crisis with aging. Mid-life crisis, says Christian psychologist and author Dr. Kevin Leman, affects women, "not just men. Particularly women who have been in the corporate side of life are bailing out." The female menopause is a crisis of its own for many women, for which Leman suggests medical help. But Leman sees the circumstances many workers of both sexes past forty find themselves in, coupled with frustrated feelings that one's job is merely "beating my head against the wall" as the real issue.

Say you're fiftysomething, you have spent a quarter of a century climbing your company's promotion ladder, then your department is reorganized and you're out looking for work.

In the next few days you face several dozen receptionists whom you swear could be schoolmates of your teen granddaughter. The several personnel managers whom you do get interviews with impress you as having as much maturity as Jerry Lewis in an old Martin and Lewis comedy. It's not long before you've begun to view yourself as on the way to imitating that old man in the cracked shoes on the fat-tired bicycle.

Or take a more mundane scenario: Your job is secure, but that's all that can be said for it. No more promotions await you, and years earlier you reached a plateau of efficiency past which it seems you have little to learn in this company.

Subtle, but also deadly to becoming a godly grandparent, is yielding to the temptation to flaunt one's financial success. We may buy a larger house or a fancy van—with a bumper sticker boasting, "I'm spending my grandchildren's inheritance!"—or even a new set of golf clubs, not because we need the extra room to entertain our families, the big car to take them picnicking, or the set of clubs so that we can fellowship with our teen grandkids on the golf course. Too often, it's our way of showing the neighbors how successful we are. And it's a means to prove to ourselves that we're not getting older, just better. After all, the ads tell us, you've worked hard—you "deserve" a $30,000 luxury car.

Time was, the agrarian society that most of America left behind by the middle of the twentieth century had built-in cushions so that old folks could just be old without feeling cheated out of life's rewards. My dad, who was born in 1916, recalled that when he was a child, a man was expected to grow a beard and walk with a cane when he reached fifty. There was then a dignity that came with age in an era when you could still find a hoary-headed Civil War veteran among the codgers on the park bench in the town square. A man of mature years can achieve significance in an agricultural setting, where the success of his farming operation is apparent, where his children are about him, offering support and encouragement in a more tangible way than in today's urban, mobile culture.

My paternal grandfather, for example, turned the reins of the operation over to my dad at age sixty-nine. From then on, until his death at eighty-four, Grandpa could view with pride his son's success in managing the farm his father had built, as they lived together, surrounded by children and grandchildren in the house Grandpa had built before Dad's birth—and where both lived until they died.

My grandmothers, too, though both had worked for a time outside the home as schoolteachers, were comfortable in their acceptance of maturity and in becoming grandmothers. Their lives centered in their homes, their kitchens, their husbands, their children, their families. When the constraints of age made it impossible for them to do heavy housework or to help in their husbands' farming or storekeeping, they could knit and sew in their rockers without any basic change in occupations. They were *still* housewives, albeit widowed. For them, there *was* no crisis.

There's a lesson here. Men or women in middle age, just beginning to become grandparents, should take stock of how they can honestly expect to spend the next thirty or forty years. This is not presuming on God. Rather, it's honestly, "If the Lord will," making plans subject to God's right to change our direction (James 4:15). With the life expectancy of Americans of either sex who've lived to become grandparents past eighty, the prudent grandparent considers that the future may hold for him thirty or forty years yet.

For some facing mid-life crisis, one solution may be in entrepreneurship, suggests Leman. Such a person "shows the grandchildren that in America you can go out on your own and do something entrepreneural," he says, noting that control over one's schedule and the satisfaction of building a business is "a good trade-off" for making less money than a salaried job.

Special training to develop latent skills will make your services valuable through middle age on into old age. One lady I know developed her talents as a seamstress, and eventually she was making custom-tailored suits out of her home. When her fingers became too stiff to operate a sewing machine, she ran a small business supplying coffee and doughnuts at break time to industrial plants nearby.

A farmer past retirement age sold his herd of milk cows. He continued to raise market crops, but his winter months were idle, so he took up an avocation he'd abandoned half a century earlier—repairing radios. After a home-study course in TV repair, he easily landed a job repairing TVs and stereos with a repair service. Free from having to milk his herd seven days a week, he and his wife now traveled often to visit grandchildren, yet he had a paycheck to carry him through lean times.

Several temptations await the grandparent caught in mid-life crisis, some of which, once yielded to, can have lifelong reverberations. King David, when he ought to have been finding his significance in leading his troops into battle, found himself spying on a young woman taking a bath, with whom he subsequently committed adultery (see 2 Sam. 11:1-4). Elijah the prophet, successful in beating the priests of Baal and so mighty in prayer that God withheld or sent rain at his request, found himself in the midst of depression, alone under a juniper tree, wanting to die. The euphoria of success was gone. Elijah took his eyes off the Lord, focused on his circumstances—a woman, Queen Jezebel, wanted his life—and he drew into himself in self pity.

"Women need to know that men need a lot of reaffirming," says Leman. "The physical area of life during those mid-life years" needs attention. "Women need it, as well," he affirms.

It's all too easy for couples to grow apart as they age, especially if they move in different circles because of job circumstances. Bitterness and habitual crankiness may ensue. Loving, joyful sexual relations become seldom. Adultery may follow as one or the other spouse seeks to reaffirm his or her youth and personal worth in an exciting, attentive bed partner. Divorce is the final step, and little is left afterwards to give the grandchildren, for we seem to have proven ourselves unable to be "more than conquerors" in Christ (Rom. 8:37).

This is not to say that those grandparents who have been divorced must accept defeat. Repentance and confession always bring restoration of fellowship with the Lord. God will renew opportunities to minister to our grandchildren as we return to him.

We too easily blame teens for sexual promiscuity, forgetting that our culture has placed its Satanic lust traps where Christians of all ages, grandparents included, can fall into them. Occasionally, in walking through the fields of life, I trip over a stone, and while nursing a bruised toe, I observe the vermin which crawl out. One such "stone" caught my attention recently when I picked up a magazine in a library intending to read an article featured on the cover. An ad for men's trousers portrayed a lean, gray haired, craggy-faced, sixtysomething male model on a chaise lounge. Seated at his feet was a girl of perhaps nineteen. Pouting, voluptuous, and spilling out of her chemise, she awaited his attention.

Feeling sorry for yourself, Grandpa? Buy yourself a new pair of slacks. Fantasize while you wear them.

Nor do grandmas escape sexual traps. As a substitute teacher I found a girl of fourteen reading a book from the public library, "with my mother's permission," she said. If the pornographic, explicit sex in that book is typical of today's popular fiction (and it is), grandmas who read books—or watch soap operas—must kick over quite a few stones, too.

Not that out-and-out adultery is the only consequence of feeding one's mind on this stuff. How many millions of couples have their relationship harmed by sins of the heart and mind that are an offense to the Lord! The sexual references in the Song of Solomon, by contrast, are designed to lead couples closer together.

Jack Wyrtzen has been widowed, and he is now married to a former widow, Joan. The Wyrtzens together have twenty-one grandchildren spread across two continents. Jack says that the secret to maintaining relationships with one another and victory over temptation is a regular, daily, quiet time where God speaks to us through his Word and we speak to God in prayer.

Forty years ago a young evangelist turned from eating supper in a Maine farmhouse to sign his name and a Scripture reference in the autograph book of a teen boy temporarily crippled by a hit-and-run driver. "Three chapters a day" he wrote with a flourish of a fountain pen after noting, "Phil. 2:16."

That evangelist signed his name "Jack Wyrtzen." I was that boy. I confess there have been lapses in that regimen. But a dozen years ago at forty, when I found myself, an English teacher and former preacher, out of work because of the closing of the college where I taught, it was the Word, particularly the books of Job and Psalms, which sustained me in my personal crisis.

Avoid focusing on the constraints of your aging process if you wish to be a positive role model for your grandchildren. It's not enough merely to avoid complaining about your aches and pains to others. Instead, positively focus on the opportunities maturity has brought you. Here are some examples:

◆

Retirement brings greater
opportunity to do good to others.

"I spent the first sixty-five years of my life working for myself and my family. Now I'm trying to do things for others," Marion Lahr told me. When I met him, Lahr, widowed two years earlier and retired from many years as a mechanical engineer, was rejoicing in the Lord as he served as construction engineer for the Dandya Leprosarium near Maradi, a remote town in Niger, sub-Sahara Africa. His full life since his year as a short-term missionary with SIM International has included supervising housing construction for Habitat for Humanity and singing with Twelve Men of Praise. As evangelical missions have broadened their ministries to include relief work, especially since the 1984 famine in Ethiopia, the need for retirees such as Lahr for short-term missionary work has increased many times.

Helping those in genuine need helps you avoid becoming a doting grandparent, spoiling grandchildren with unappreciated gifts. Not a few grandparents have been disappointed when a grandson or granddaughter abused a car the grandparents gave, wasted a gift of money, or wrecked an expensive garment intended for special occasions. The grandparent who seeks to meet genuine needs will not be thought indulgent and will learn to lovingly tailor his giving to real needs as the Lord lays them on his heart.

I recall that one of the last letters I ever received from my grandmother contained a check for ten dollars. I was a senior in college and my grandfather, her husband of forty-five years, had died months earlier. The money was the tithe of Grandpa's $100 life insurance policy. The only other gift I can specifically recall receiving from her was a modestly expensive flannel shirt when I was in the seventh grade. I had never owned a "store-boughten" shirt, except hand-me-downs, and I had requested this for my birthday. Grandma was not an indulgent woman, but she was giving. The life-insurance money from my newly widowed grandmother was received like an alabaster box of precious ointment, I assure you.

◆

Romance is another
hedge against growing old.

If your spouse is living, keep your love romantic by doing special things for him or her daily. Read the *Song of Solomon* together. Go for walks together. Plan times away from home when the two of you can be alone together. We too easily wish to include other family members in affairs that ought to be private, forgetting that it's out of times together that the ability to confidently relate to our grandchildren arises.

When we become too busy to go off for a weekend in a motel, to rent a boat for a leisurely Saturday ride, or to stop at that special ice cream parlor—just the two of you—for an unhurried cone, relationships tend to become inverted.

As a young pastor in rural Maine I was called to visit in the home of an elderly couple, where the wife's mother had recently died. The aged matriarch was laid out in her coffin in a small bedroom off the parlor. After the gray-haired wife, herself past seventy, had ushered me by her mother's casket, I inquired politely, "How old was your mother?"

"Ninety-three."

"I'm sorry you lost her," I answered.

" 'Bout time!" growled the son-in-law from his seat in the corner. This gentleman, nearly eighty, had for years suffered under not having his wife to himself. Not given to creative ways of finding time alone with his wife, he was relieved, for what then seemed to me selfish reasons, that she could now give him some attention.

Neither husband nor wife in this case had learned to cultivate the other's attention, I'm afraid. Saddled by circumstances, she had become a care-worn old woman and he an old grouch.

"At eighty-five I feel like a young man in my thirties or forties," says Ivan Green. Ivan and his bride, Eva, eighty, were married recently after being widowed from marriages totaling more than 100 years. They had had happy first marriages, and since their spouses had passed on, they had both kept busy making others happy. Eva was visiting friends in a nursing home when Ivan, a retired minister, came by to conduct a chapel service. After the service, Eva and Ivan were introduced. "He kissed me and swept me off my feet," recalls Eva.

Today, the Greens are "like two teenagers in love," says one of Eva's daughters. Adds Eva, "We have a wonderful life" together. "We're still honeymooning."

Not all can remarry, certainly; nor should all remarry who can. But whether you have been with your mate fifty years or you're newlyweds of fifty weeks, keeping romance alive will model a positive, uplifting life before your grandchildren.

◆

Exercise is another hedge
against growing old.

Fourteen million Americans past age fifty-five have discovered that walking will "produce a happier frame of mind" says syndicated columnist Evelyn Sullivan. A brisk walk, says Sullivan, can release tension and stress, elevate moods, and alleviate depression. Many grandparents who walk thirty minutes a day "insist that walking just makes them feel good," she says.

I took my two-year-old granddaughter for a walk the other day after her persistence dragged me from my easy chair. It was Sunday, and I'd spent the morning sitting in a pew, then sitting for dinner, then sitting to read. Her small legs moved at a trot while my long ones ambled at a leisurely pace. Soon, though, she spied the back-yard swing and, "Grandpa, push me!" was all her delight.

I returned refreshed from that stroll with little Katy. I'm not sure if it was the exercise or the social interaction with my granddaughter that lifted my spirits. But I know I was six feet tall when I left for that walk. In Katy's estimation, I was seven feet tall when we returned.

◆

*Intellectual stimulation is
another hedge against growing old.*

That "You can't teach an old dog new tricks" is only true when the dog refuses to learn. Remko Slagter, 101, graduated from Fruitport (Michigan) High School in 1992, thirty years after he retired from a career laying bricks. Slagter, whose native tongue is Dutch, immigrated to the U.S. from The Netherlands in 1910. He was 97 when he enrolled in high school, and he continues to take high-school classes as a postgraduate student.

More than 1,600 colleges and universities and special schools nationwide offer special courses for senior citizens over age fifty-five, many of them free. For instance, The Academy of Lifelong Learning, Wilmington, Delaware, has 1,500 students studying courses ranging from Beethoven to Understanding the Legal System. The school's assistant coordinator, Robert Robinson, says that "instead of going to a nursing home, these people have decided to pursue learning and cultural aggrandizement." Student Roxana Arsht, seventy-six, a retired judge, agrees. "We want to learn," says Arsht. "We're alive, and we don't want to get stale."

Old minds don't get "stale" when they're regularly nourished by intellectual fodder. Well-fed minds avoid the all-too-common condition of being left behind by the grandchildren when they become teens.

◆

*Grandparents who dress with
dignity tend to earn the respect
of their grandchildren.*

In my mother's album of family pictures stretching back more than a century is a snapshot of my grandparents. Grandpa wears a three-piece suit of summer flannel, complete with high-laced dress shoes, his outfit topped with a straw boater. Grandma is wearing a rather fancy flowing dress, beads, and gloves; like Grandpa, she sports a straw hat, tied down with a silk scarf. They are seated on a blanket, a wicker picnic basket opened before them. This is no studio portrait. The picture, from about 1920, was taken on the beach!

The revolution in clothing styles since that photo was taken has more to do with the propriety of certain clothes to certain occasions than with actual style changes. Grandpa's suit of three-quarters of a century back would hardly turn a head in a business office or a church even today. But as beachwear?

As mature grandparents, though, we must consider more than style and propriety. We recognize that aging, often portly bodies require more subtle disguising with carefully arranged drapery than our grandchildren's lithe figures need. One advantage though—we can spend more for our clothes and make them last longer!

Today's grandfathers *do* wear jogging suits when they exercise. Grandmas wear jeans and sandals to picnics. They wear bathing suits on beaches. But the wise grandparent is perceptive enough to realize that certain clothes designed for the young are not suited for fiftysomethings in public. A polo shirt can grotesquely accentuate a less-than-flat male belly, for instance.

A lady friend, who once ran a successful ladies' clothing store in Manhattan, tells me that the woman who wants to be thought a lady wears calf-length skirts in public. Pantsuits are for secretaries; skirted suits are worn by business ladies who wish to be taken seriously, of any age. The same goes for a white or pin-striped shirt and tie for men in business.

◆

A *healthy sense* *of humor*

will not only open the hearts of your grandchildren, but it may enable you to live healthier and longer, too. "A merry heart doeth good like a medicine" (Prov. 17:22) is advice octogenarian Jack Wyrtzen, founder of Word of Life, an international ministry for *youth,* is fond of repeating.

Can you chuckle when ten-month-old Jennifer dumps her Cheerios on your newly carpeted kitchen floor? As her mother, unperturbed, remarks dryly, "Your new wet 'n' dry vac'll take it up, Mom" you recall that you waited until the kids were grown to get the kitchen carpeted. Do you maintain your ability to smile and smooth things over when your out-of-state children, with seven kids under seven among them, have camped in your family room, living room, and master bedroom for three days over the Fourth of July, and the three families who have invaded your domain have got on each other's nerves over conflicting discipline philosophies (you and Grandpa are bunking in your son-in-law's pop-up camper)? And can you keep your humor as you work with two recipes of pancake batter because the family from Ohio wants buckwheat in their flapjacks, but the ones from Georgia abhor buckwheat and insist on corn meal? Thankfully, the family from New Jersey eats them either way.

Is it true that folks who laugh a lot live longer? I know of no conclusive study, so I jotted down the names of ten comedians, past and present. In the order they occurred to me, with their ages in 1992, or age at death, these are: Jackie Gleason, 71; Bob Hope, 89; Jimmy Durante, 87; Art Carney, 74; Groucho Marx, 87; George Burns, 96; Lawrence Welk, 89 (Welk was a musician, but his joking manner is known to millions of grandparents); Minnie Pearl, 80; Arthur Godfrey, 80; Jack Benny, 80. Of those in this list who died youngest, two (Jackie Gleason, 71, and Jack Benny, 80) had diabetes. Minnie Pearl, at 80, has diabetes. Art Carney, included in the list at a "young" 74, is still living. Burns and Hope are still working!

A grandfather of my acquaintance, a man who, like some in the list above had several bad habits hurtful to his health, spent many years as a Maine rural mail carrier. When he died past eighty he was mourned by the entire community, for his habit of wisecracking with his patrons at their mailboxes had captured the hearts of his townsfolk. Carl "Happy" Drake is likely his town's best-loved citizen even a quarter century after his death. Importantly, Carl Drake, as well as the comedians mentioned, made *others* happy. An important job of a grandparent is to give the grandchildren—and their parents—practical lessons in happiness.

I think I know now why I was so fond of my maternal grandmother, an affection that lasted from my childhood until her death shortly after the birth of my eldest child, her first great-granddaughter. She was a quiet, unassuming woman known for her kindness and generosity. And Grandma Fuller had a sense of humor. When she opened her mouth it was often in mirth, sometimes to tell a funny story like the one about the time her mother-in-law caught a skunk that was robbing her henhouse by the tail. The poor woman bathed in tomato juice to remove the odor. But burying her clothes didn't kill the stink!

7

Things Not Found in Books

When I was a child I can remember being admonished not to peek in Grandma's knitting bag during the weeks before Christmas. After the supper dishes were cleared away and we children were tucked in bed by Mother, Grandma would knit in her rocker. Thick woolen socks and mittens she made, not the cheap, store-bought kind with loops inside to snag your fingers, but substantial stuff that would keep a fellow's hands warm even after an hour of throwing snowballs.

Grandma knew what was in her bag, and she kept it secret. And she knew how many knits and purls were needed to make a boy's mittens, though I never knew her to use a pattern. Like all good grandparents, mine knew a myriad of things, from practical skills such as knitting, to family tales passed down through generations, to spiritual truths learned in a life of maturing and growing in Christ.

◆

Tolerance, for instance, is an important secret known to grandparents

which they can share with their grandkids. My wife tells how her grandmother taught her by example and precept to accept and love those with physical deformities. She learned not to laugh at an old man's stoop, nor shun a person with a missing limb, nor tease a child who stutters.

Uncle Willis, though not himself a grandparent, was of my grandmother's generation. He hired me, a teen, to help fix his fences, and we took his pickup truck to the backside of his farm, where a sheep-wire fence bordered his pasture next to the woods. I soon found him aggravating to work with, for he was slow. Not slow and meticulous—that I could have appreciated. Uncle Willis was plain slow, and I wanted to get on to more interesting tasks.

"You know how old this fence is?" he chuckled eventually.

"Twenty years," I ventured, careful to predate my own time.

"I helped my father build it before I went to war."

I visualized then an old photo of him in his American Expeditionary Force uniform before he followed General Pershing to France. His "war" was the First World War. His fence was new in 1917.

◆

Having lived over time,
grandparents can measure time.

I learned to see time in a broader perspective from Uncle Willis that day. They know that many of the things youth hurries for are not worth the bother.

"What are those?" I asked Mother's Uncle Oscar one spring afternoon. He had been for a tramp in the woods. A trapper, Uncle Oscar knew every acre of the forest for miles around, so I wasn't surprised to see his hand-woven, Indian-style wicker knapsack full of woodland herbs.

"Fiddleheads," he explained. "Young ferns."

Here were hundreds of these pale-green, fuzzy plants. And I knew that Uncle Oscar was not a gourmet who gathered these succulents to please a jaded palate. Rather, I learned frugality from Uncle Oscar, in the same session that I learned that the springtime woods holds hidden good food for the one who will venture forth. He was a widower, a lean, healthy man whose appetites and needs were as sparse as his stature. A colonial Virginia planter, William Byrd, once observed that he could carry a shilling in his pocket for a month without need to spend it. I'm sure Uncle Oscar could have done the same with a quarter!

◆

Grandparents know family
history and stories

that are part of the stuff of their family's goodly heritage. Such history, related in proper detail, can help give direction and maturity, as an older child or teen learns to appreciate who he is in a context of where he came from.

Until my manhood, my family's history, except for photo albums and Grandpa's terse diary entries, was entirely oral. Then an aunt, herself a grandmother, began writing a history of our community. In the process she collected bits and pieces of family lore, as well as a family tree researched back over 400 years.

Some of Aunt Ruby's material she copied and shared with other family members. Other information she published as a softcover book, *As I Remember.*

Meanwhile, my mother put together a typewritten collection of her memories over three quarters of a century. And my sister expanded Aunt Ruby's genealogical records through library research of her own.

But I think the most fascinating story of all was told me and brother George by Grandpa Wiggin when we both were small: the story of "The First Wiggin Who Came to America." When Grandpa was a child, he had relatives living whose lives reached back to the eighteenth century, and he evidently heard this tale from one of them.

Tom Wiggin, born in England in 1592, was kidnapped at age fourteen (1606) and brought to Maine, to the mouth of the Penobscot River, where the ship anchored by the riverbank for the night. Next morning, young Tom was given an axe and sent up the rigging to cut a mast free from overhanging pine limbs. Instead, he swung himself ashore and escaped into the forest. The Lord preserved him, and he managed to get back to England, possibly with fishermen who had wintered on the New England coast to dry codfish. He returned to America as captain of his own vessel to settle in New Hampshire about 1628.

Perhaps your grandchildren would be thrilled to hear of their ancestors' trip on a steamship and their stop at Ellis Island, as thrilled as I was when I listened as a friend told of her father's journey as a young man to America from Germany. Or perhaps, like my wife's family, your family's history disappears into the mists of the Great Smoky Mountains where Catherine Marshall's *Christy* is set, early in the twentieth century. Whatever you may know of your family's past, especially its Christian heritage, can help give your grandchildren a sense of who they are and a sense of direction for coming years.

Christian psychologist Kevin Leman recommends that grandparents do a " 'This is your Life,' minus Ralph Edwards." Set up a video camera and "talk to your grandchildren and describe your life, your parents, your grandparents, where they came from, what was important to them, and how you got to where you are in life," Leman suggests. He recommends that the tape be put with your will and other important papers, not to be played back until you have died.

*A major knowledge grandparents
have not found in books is maturity,*

with its many lessons, practical, moral, and spiritual.
And the truly mature grandparent is also the wise man or
woman who realizes that maturity doesn't come auto-
matically with age, though when we were children we no
doubt thought so. Job observed that though "multitude of
years should teach wisdom, . . . the aged (do not always)
understand judgment" (Job 32:7 and 9).

When I think of maturity, my mind goes to J. Oswald
Sanders, an elder statesman of Christian missions and
author of some forty devotional books, whom I interviewed on the subject of Christian maturity at Gull Lake
Bible Conference. But years earlier, Sanders, who for a
time filled the shoes of J. Hudson Taylor as director of
the China Inland Mission Overseas Missionary Fellowship (SIM/OMF), was fifty-three and I a teenager, when
I first heard him speak. It amazes me that I now am a
grandfather of fifty-three as I write this, and Sanders has
recently passed away (he was nearly 90!).

J. Oswald Sanders was general director of CIM, and I
a high-school student of seventeen when I heard him
speak at a missionary conference at New Brunswick
Bible Institute, in Canada. His speaking delivery was
direct and forceful—the kind of message at which one
either squirmed in conviction or mocked in rebellion. I
squirmed.

Sanders' text then was Romans 10:9, "That if thou shalt confess with thy mouth *Jesus as Lord* (Scofield marginal rendering), and shalt believe in thine heart that God hath raised him from the dead, thou shalt be saved." He preached that if "Christ is not Lord of all, He is not Lord at all." As a child of nine I had surrendered my heart to Christ. He had been Lord of my life, but as a teen I had toyed with the notion that one could believe and be saved and bound for heaven, living above moral sin, but pretty much leading a self-directed life otherwise. God opened my heart with Sanders' preaching. Christ had to be Lord of my life without reservation. I had lingered between two opinions long enough. I had begun the long march (not without its backward steps) toward Christian maturity.

A third of a century passed before I heard J. Oswald Sanders preach again. This time I sat down front in a crowd that numbered only a few dozen, compared with more than a thousand when he had been in his heyday. Maturity in Christ does not demand that its ego be massaged by an ever-larger audience. The man who had seemed stern and severe when he had been my age now was a gentle grandfather in a cardigan. "Let us go on unto maturity," he read from his text. *Would my own maturity require as many years again since I last heard him preach?* I wondered. Then he said something which startled me: "If He is not Lord of all, He is not Lord at all," his mellow voice intoned, emphasizing his familiar refrain as the starting point in a search for Christian maturity. Truth, which does not change with God, will not change in the hands of God's man!

As a young lawyer in New Zealand, J. Oswald Sanders was also beginning to be known for his ability to teach the Bible, he told me later as we sat facing each other in his room. Those were the years of the Great Depression, and his audience one day was a prayer group of ladies whose husbands were out of work.

"Mr. Sanders will be all right as a speaker when he's suffered a little," remarked a lady afterward. But as a lawyer, and the son of a well-to-do attorney, Sanders had always been pretty much insulated from the harshness of the workaday world, and he knew this.

Maturity requires time and experience, J. Oswald Sanders was to learn. Not all folks, however, mature at the same rate, nor do all profit equally from the same kinds of experiences, Sanders told me. "It takes God only three months to grow a squash but a hundred years to grow an oak," he chuckled. "Which would you rather be?"

J. Oswald Sanders enumerated for me several steps to Christian maturity which grandparents can apply to their own lives in order to lead their grandchildren into maturity. "The most potent hindrance to spiritual maturity," he said, is "a failure to maintain a consistent devotional life." In the morning, if you can do it, "feed on the Word of God. Fellowship with him through prayer and worship," he said.

My godly paternal grandfather had to begin milking his cows at five o'clock, so morning devotions were not feasible. But I can still see him in the evening by his library table in the light of a kerosene lamp, fountain pen in hand, his Bible and diary on the wide maple arm of his chair. Though family devotions were irregular at our house, seeing Grandpa—and since then both my children's grandfathers—read his Bible in the lamplight has impressed me with the importance of being consistent in the Word.

I have Grandpa's Bible now. It is a 1917 Thompson, rebound shortly before his death. Hardly a page is without one of his markings, and here and there are outlines or notes scribbled in the margins.

I had not seen that old book for some thirty years, and it had passed through several family members before it came to me. Tucked inside as a bookmark was the answer to an old enigma. I had once seen a strip of old photo-booth snapshots of my grandfather, cut in half lengthwise. What was on the other half? I found it in his Bible: Grandma Wiggin's photos, four of them, were that bookmark! On the reverse in his handwriting was this note: "October 1, 1925. Always love, I will remember you."

The Grandma Wiggin who is my wife is today about the same age as Grandpa's wife, the Grandma Wiggin of my childhood. Like me, he had two loves—the Word of God and the woman God had given him. And he'd cut the strip photo apart, given Grandma the half with his photos, then kept hers with his dearest possession!

◆

*Grandparents know what things
to hold dear in life.*

As the years pass, we learn to narrow these to a very short list indeed!

Suffering, loss, and sorrow were to become a part of J. Oswald Sanders' experience; twice, in fact, between my first hearing him preach and the last, he lost a wife—in 1966 and again in 1972—leaving him to walk alone a road which has taken him throughout the world to minister to others. "Death is a part of life," Sanders affirmed. "But the death of one close to you may bring either bitterness or maturity, depending on how you handle it."

"Some people are so swallowed up in grief" over the loss of a loved one that they become "like the Psalmist, who said, 'My soul refused to be comforted'" (Ps. 77:2), reflected Sanders. He told of a lifelong friend who lost a wife of fifty years. "He practically threw in the towel when she died, and he was absolutely lost. This man died (in anguish) five or six years later. He went out on a minor key," Sanders observed.

Yet grief is a "necessary and important response" to death, Sanders said. "Tears often have a therapeutic effect." He told of a woman who had been recently bereaved. Told by a friend that "Sorrow does color life, doesn't it?" the woman replied, "Yes, but I intend to choose the colors." Sanders mused that "she didn't choose black and she didn't choose purple. She chose gold."

During her last three months of life, J. Oswald Sanders' first wife was in considerable pain from cancer. "The Lord lifted us above sorrow, buoying up the both of us in a very wonderful way so that we were both carried through it, and she died triumphantly," he exulted.

What things did Grandpa Wiggin know that are not found in books? I have had access to his diaries and read the stuff he has written down—most of it is mundane, maddeningly terse. The entrance for January 30, 1916, the date of my father's birth, for instance, reads, "Wind W-N-W. Boy born." That was it. No hint of who the doctor was, how the mother was doing, which relatives stopped by or phoned to congratulate the parents—no name given, even!

Grandpa has told me a bit about his past in some detail. But there was one story into which I'd always feared to pry, a story of sorrow, the story of Grandpa's little sister, commemorated in a white marble headstone: "Little Clara, how we miss you,/ Your gentle voice no more we'll hear;/ For you've left and gone to heaven,/ Where there is no pain nor care." Since he died I have learned that Grandpa carried this sorrow with him for many years, and in my own maturity I think I understand why.

Six-year-old Clara had just got over a bout with scarlet fever when brother Elmer, age eight, decided to tease her. He followed the long ell from the house to the barn, where he buried himself under the hay that raw early spring day. Clara called and called until she was hoarse, but Elmer refused to answer. Clara had a relapse from the episode. Days later, she died.

I'll never know for sure if Grandpa Elmer Wiggin ever reconciled himself to fully accept Clara's death, receiving Christ's forgiveness for his childish meanness or not. But, though reportedly he brooded over the incident for years, I've reason to believe that he did come to accept it. Years after Grandpa died a report came to me which does not seem consistent with a man whose heart lay troubled and aching all his adult life.

I was pumping gas at a country store the summer I graduated from high school. A late-model luxury car with out-of-state license plates pulled up. "Fill 'er up." Then, "What is your name, son?" inquired the dignified, well-dressed, elderly driver.

"Eric Wiggin."

"Elmer Wiggin your grandfather?"

"Yes, sir."

"When I was a small boy, your grandfather was our mail carrier. He was the kindest man I ever knew."

Grandpa Wiggin had once driven a horse-drawn R.F.D. wagon. Sometime in the years since Clara's untimely death he had matured, learned the meaning of grief, and had accepted Christ's forgiveness so that half a century later an old man would remember him for such fruits of the Spirit as gentleness and goodness shown toward a child about the age of his sister when she died.

In a message I heard him preach in his sunset years, J. Oswald Sanders points out that Christian maturity develops in the believer's life as "the Holy Spirit produces a cameo of the life of Christ" in our lives "by producing in our lives the nine fruits of the Spirit," as listed in Galatians 5:22-23. These are enumerated here, with summaries of Sanders' comments, for Christian grandparents:

1. "Love is not self centered," he said; "it's always giving. The love of God is shed abroad from our lives by the Holy Spirit" (see Rom. 5:5).
2. "Joy," said Sanders, "can exist in the deepest sorrow. True love is joyous. Are you fun to live with?"
3. "Peace" comes from "inner surrender to the will of God," he said. It is shown through "tranquility" in the midst of turmoil. "Peace is not the absence of trouble; it is the presence of God" in trouble. "Do you borrow tomorrow's trouble today so that you can get double value out of it?" he asked.
4. "Patience—it was just as much the 'now generation' when I was young as it is today. The most difficult thing is to be patient with people," and the spiritually mature person develops this trait, he said.
5. "Gentleness" is "being able to project yourself into the feelings of other people," Sanders said.
6. "Goodness" is the imitation of Christ who "went about doing good" (Acts 10:38). This is not mere-

ly being morally good, but doing good things. "How many times this week have you gone out of your way to do something kind, something good for others?" he asked.

7. "Faith" is here "faithfulness," he explained. "Jesus will not say, 'Well done, *successful* servant,' but *'faithful* servant.' "

8. "Meekness is not an invertebrate quality. Neither Jesus nor Moses was weak, though they were meek. It's the opposite of self-assertion. There is no retaliation in meekness."

9. "Temperance" is shown in "discipline in one's devotional life," Sanders affirmed.

Elisabeth Elliot, in *The Liberty of Obedience,* observes that as believers walk with the Lord, grandparents included, there is "That marvelous hope—that we *shall* yet reach that ultimate end of all creation—maturity in Christ." It is for our maturation, that we might, in maturity, measure up to "the stature of the fullness of Christ" that God works in our lives (Eph. 4:12-13). For this purpose we have been left on earth to be grandparents— for our own maturing and to aid in the maturing in Christ of the grandchildren God has given us. This is a precious secret held by believing grandparents. Can we share it with our grandchildren?

8

Busy Moms, Babysitting Grandmoms

A mother of my acquaintance gave birth to six youngsters—triplets, twins, a single birth—within three years of her marriage. Few young moms, however, have such a pressing need for a baby sitter!

But with more and more mothers joining the work force in the fifty years since American manufacturers geared up to produce armaments at the outset of World War II and this same process of industrialization pushing parents and grandparents into separate housing often miles apart, the shortage of baby sitters has become acute. Working mothers with means to do so have resorted to day-care centers. Not to be outdone by secular competition, many churches have got into the day-care business, also. And the spin-offs of this new industry have not always been pleasant.

One large church in the South that started a Christian school as a ministry to its own families added a day-care center as a missionary outreach to divorced and single mothers. Within a few years, school directors were dismayed to find that the children of divorcees admitted to the school as graduates of the pre-K program had become a disruptive element in the classroom. Secular day-care centers in one survey, however, had fewer than 20 percent of enrollees from single-parent homes. One director stated frankly that her fees were too high for single working moms to afford them.

Sexual abuse in day-care centers, while relatively rare, is a hobgoblin parents who pass their kids to somebody else's care must contend with. The California case a decade ago, for instance, in which hundreds of children were allegedly molested, gives reason for concern among parents who choose day-care.

But sex abuse can't happen in a Bible-believing church's day-care, can it? A mid-sized Midwestern evangelical church, which used teens and older children as caregivers in its nursery while parents were attending Sunday or prayer services, uncovered the case of a youth who molested sixty-four children of both sexes over a three-year period before he was caught and prosecuted. That youth was the son of the former Sunday school superintendent, who turned out to be a heavy user of pornography, to which his kids had access. As the presence of porn and the consequences of divorce pervade our society, the danger of your grandchild becoming exposed to sex abuse increases proportionately.

But consideration of exposing a child to profane company, as in a day-care overloaded with kids from broken homes, or even sexual abuse, while a real concern, misses the basic issue of day-care as an alternative for a Christian home. Grandparents and parents might well ask themselves if day-care of any kind—except in very limited circumstances where the mothers are present through much of the day—is at all a viable choice for their kids or grandkids.

◆

The factor of working mothers harks back to the massive influx of immigrants into America during the late nineteenth century.

Parochial schools and public kindergartens were established to get the kids of working mothers off the streets in those days (their grandmothers had frequently been left behind in Europe), but these families, usually through religious values and strict family discipline, eventually rose above the chaos. The working mothers of the late nineteenth century become the grandmothers of the early twentieth century, as the pattern for mothers to stay home or for grandmothers to baby-sit when mothers must work was reestablished with the help of a burgeoning American economy.

My own family has seen at least four generations of parents raising their own children, with minimal help from baby-sitting grandmoms, and we expect this pattern to continue. Both my grandmothers, for instance, returned to their mothers' homes for the births of my parents or aunts. Though Mother seldom left her children in the care of either grandmother, except when she was recuperating from another childbirth, Grandma Wiggin's turn to tend grandchildren came fifteen years into my parents' marriage when Dad's farming operation folded and he and Mother took employment in a bakery.

There were five of us then, and we were all in school. I can still recall Grandma's reaction to after-school differences of opinion between me and my brothers: she would retreat to her room and shut the door. She had raised three children of her own, whose births were spread over twenty three years—five at once were a bit more than Grandma could take. Dad would settle with us when he and Mother got home!

Times with Grandma Fuller, our maternal grandmother, were much more pleasant, for she would agree to care for only one of us at a time, usually; two at most.

Mother quit her bakery job after a year, but she continued to raise extra cash as an Avon lady. The Lord blessed her with two more children right after Dad found a better job as a carpenter. But Grandma's baby-sitting was still infrequent; Mother simply trundled her latest baby along with her on her Avon route.

Dot and I began our family upstairs above my parents, and Mother was occasionally the baby sitter for our two oldest. A grandma by now, Mother was still an Avon Lady. I recall that we sometimes had to arrange our times alone around Grandma's schedule as a saleslady. A move to Indiana put us across the street from a sister-in-law, and Dot sometimes traded baby-sitting with her. A year later Mother followed us, and again we had

Grandma Wiggin as a baby sitter, this time just around the block.

We now live in Michigan, four hours from our oldest granddaughter, in Indiana, so our daughter, little Katy's mother, now sometimes calls on Great-grandma Wiggin to baby-sit. On occasions when Katy and her parents visit us, you can bet that Grandma Wiggin (my wife, Dot) jealously guards her time so she can spend it with Katy.

Grandmothers who offer their services as baby sitters so that married daughters or daughters-in-law with small children can work out of the home full time may be contributing to the instability of the next generation, while helping the family little with the budget, if any. The dictum, "Give me a child until he is seven, and he will always be a Catholic" (Ignatius Loyola) has universal application, I believe. Mothers need to be with their children during their first seven years of life, for it is in these years that basic values and attitudes are formed. Hannah, the mother of the great prophet Samuel, reared him until he was seven before placing him in the priest's hands for training in temple service (see 1 Sam. 1:24-28). Jesus continued to be "subject unto" his mother Mary and stepfather Joseph even after age twelve (see Luke 2:42-52). Such added costs as the need for an extra car, work clothes, prepared foods, and more frequent restaurant meals can easily add up to its being cheaper for the frugal mother to stay home and enjoy her children and let them enjoy her.

Mothers at home can often do much to help the family budget, however. And grandmothers can gently nudge them in this direction when the mother is receptive to advice. Better attention to budgeting and such traditional household arts as meal preparation from scratch, sewing, and gardening should be encouraged. Grandma can (and should!) stop by with a casserole or kettle of soup now and then. Both grandparents can help with the gardening, perhaps planting enough for themselves also. Sometimes Grandpa can help by using his mechanical skills to repair an auto or a furnace, saving a young family from budget-busting emergencies which might push a mother of young children into taking a job.

Too, some mothers have found work-at-home projects, ranging from making sweaters on an automatic knitting machine to computer programming. One mother has encouraged her pre-teens to take on extensive paper routes, and she helps them and shares the profits.

Mothers should be cautious of work-at-home projects widely advertised in newspapers, however, since many of these are out-and-out frauds. Instead, investigate what books and pamphlets your library has on starting home-based small businesses.

Homemade Business, by Donna Partow, available from Focus on the Family Publishing, 1 (800) A-FAMILY, has ideas for 200 home-based businesses, worksheets, and testimonies by mothers who have stayed home, and helped their families' cash flow, as well. Also worth checking out is *Home Businesses Under $5,000,* a primer on how to start and run a home business. Send

$5.50 to Sim Features, Box 368, Cardiff, CA 92007. And *Homework Newsletter,* written from a Christian perspective, is $20 a year, at P.O. Box 394 Simsbury, CT 06070; sample issue $3. These three were featured in *Focus on the Family,* June 1992. Mother and Grandma may even find themselves partners in a well-paying venture!

◆

How much a grandmother can or should sit with a grandchild depends largely on your circumstances, and those of the married children.

If Grandma herself is employed, then her times of baby-sitting will necessarily be limited by her work hours. If a daughter is divorced or widowed and needs to work to support herself and her child(ren), then Grandma will probably be the natural resort to give home care.

Grandmothers can add much to a young family's happiness by sharing the load on an endless assortment of occasions—from taking care of an infant or toddler while Mom goes to the laundromat, to keeping several grandchildren while Mom and Dad take a second honeymoon.

But if Mom (daughter or daughter-in-law) wants you to help them out so she can take a job—to buy new furniture, a nicer or a second car, adult recreational toys (boats, snowmobiles, etc.), it's probably wisest to firmly resist and urge her and her husband to seek Christian financial counselling before such a decision is made. One young Christian father went to his pastor after his wife had taken their two kids home to Grandma and sued for divorce. About a year earlier, after he'd gotten a raise, at his insistence they traded their cozy, older, three-bedroom house for a new, four-bedroom house with two baths and a two-stall garage. The old furniture looked shabby in new surroundings, so new furniture was bought on credit. Then the wife went to work to meet the furniture payments, putting the kids in day-care.

"I didn't want this house and furniture in the first place," she wrote in a note she left behind; "I wanted a family!"

Christian financial counselors Ron Blue and Larry Burkett both have written several books available in Christian bookstores or your church's library to help young parents through such money squeezes. Burkett's office recommends *The Complete Financial Guide for Young Couples* as a starter. This and other Burkett titles can be mail ordered by phoning Christian Financial Concepts at 1 (800) 722-1976.

But wait! Why have things gotten to the point that a young mother would want to turn preschool kids over to Grandma while she works? This is not a "What might have been" caveat. Rather, what can you do now?

Let's go to the point of need, a new washing machine for $500, perhaps. You've wanted one for years, but your old one is still working well. Give the family yours when you buy a new one. But you can do better. Buy that new washer for your kids who have young children and need it more than you do. Keep the old one yourself, if you can't afford both—ours is twenty-two years old; for its first eighteen years it served an elderly lady who lived alone! Or, some grandmas simply invite the daughter or daughter-in-law over for a twice-weekly laundry and help with the folding and ironing while helping tend the youngsters.

Subscribe to a diaper service for that young mother, and pay for it yourself. That's about $70 a month, versus $45 to $75 monthly for disposable diapers. Or, if Mom's agreeable to it, spring $50 up front for four dozen cloth diapers and a box of laundry soap.

◆

Somehow, American Christians have gotten away from an important Bible principle so common in Asian cultures, that of family members helping each other.

The concept of kicking the kids out of the nest early and making them rugged individualists is not found in Scripture. "Give, and it shall be given unto you," Christ stressed in his *Sermon on the Mount* (Luke 6:38). Give to your grandchildren's needs, and you can expect to be "given unto" in return, in the form of grandchildren who will love you in your old age.

Too often we perceive that we are to give to the church or to the poor, so we may do so to the exclusion of needy family members. The strongest Bible teaching about giving points out that Christians should help other members of the family of God (see 2 Cor. 8–9); and this should include family members in need. Parents are to help children and grandchildren (see 2 Cor. 12:14). The custom of hanging on to all you've got until you die, then leaving it to loved ones in your will has robbed many a grandparent of the blessing of helping their grandkids, directly or through their parents in this life (see Matt. 10:42).

Caring for older children after school hours is a matter largely dependent on the logistics of getting the kids to your house after school either by bus, foot or bicycle, or in your auto. Grandma Hackney, my wife's mother, served as a surrogate grandmother over many years for a child who attended school just a five-minute walk from her house. He stopped at her house for soup and sandwiches until his father could pick him up after work. This young man now has a bond with Grandma Hackney possibly as strong as most natural ties.

If you have built loving bonds with your grandchildren while they were small, stopping by Grandma's house on the way home will come naturally to them. Grandma's home can also serve as a place where an ill child can receive care if he takes sick at school, if this is cleared in advance with school officials.

Should you charge for your baby-sitting services for grandchildren? Whenever money changes hands within a family, in either direction, it should be based on need, not as a business arrangement. Parents who can afford to and wish to may pay, of course. Perhaps you might wish to budget that money for birthday or Christmas gifts later. In the case of Grandma Hackney's caring for a non-relative, she was paid weekly for a service which saved his family a good deal of money; they both were working and could afford it, and she needed the money. You may wish to help a family from your church in difficult circumstances with some gratis baby-sitting, of course.

Details of baby-sitting with grandchildren, therefore, need to be mutually worked out in a loving context of family members helping each other. Does the *need* exist? Have all the options been explored? What will be best for the children? What arrangement will best assure that your spiritual and cultural heritage will be passed on to your grandchildren, rather than be undermined by secular programs often subtly contrary to godly values?

9

The Split-Family Grandparent

A dark family secret when I was growing up was that, years before I was born, Great-aunt Marcia had been divorced. I learned of this family skeleton only after reading of her prior marriage in an antiquated statistical report! Of the fifteen families that lived on our country lane when I was a teen, only two of the couples, 13 percent, had ever been divorced, though the divorce of a son in another community had touched one family in our neighborhood. Divorce, in those days, was a matter of family shame and extreme embarrassment.

Many grandparents reading this book, like the couples I knew as a child, have never been divorced. But my contact in recent times with Christian families indicates that more than half of today's grandparents have one or more divorced sons or daughters, perhaps the parents of several of your grandchildren. For example, I often meet pastors or Christian leaders, sometimes of national prominence, who have a divorced son or daughter.

One in two marriages has ended in divorce since 1981, up from one in three thirty years ago. The divorce rate jumped 40 percent in the dozen years after forty-eight states, beginning with California in 1969, passed no-fault divorce laws. The rate has since leveled off.

One-third of all American children currently live in single-parent homes, and 60 percent will spend part of their growing-up years with a divorced or unmarried mother, according to a January 15, 1992 report by Louis W. Sullivan, U. S. Secretary of Health and Human Services. While no study exists to show what percentages of Christian grandparents have divorced children and grandchildren living with only one parent, these shocking statistics would indicate that it's a problem many of us do, or eventually will, face.

The responsibility which a grandparent must bear, especially toward a divorced daughter or granddaughter, is great indeed. A report in *The Family in America* (June 1992) states that divorced women and their children experience a 73 percent decline in their standard of living, on average, during the first year after the divorce. Compounding this, no-fault divorce laws have virtually eliminated alimony, and these laws so burden both parents that the family home must often be sold, and the mother and children must move. The choice for such a mother is frequently between moving herself and her children in with her parents or moving into government-subsidized project housing with attendant high crime and rowdy neighbors. And it's likely she'll need a job and will call upon the grandparents to baby-sit, whether she lives with them or not. The same report states that children of divorce are half again as likely to repeat a grade in school as those from two-parent homes. These kids are 70 percent more likely to get expelled from school and far more likely to drop out without graduating.

Remarriage sometimes, though not always, compounds the problem. Runaways are more likely to come from homes with a stepparent or live-in boyfriend than from either two- (natural) parent homes or single-parent homes. The problem of sexual molestation, of epidemic proportions in the 1990s, also most commonly involves a mother's second marriage or cohabitation, though media reports have tended to highlight cases involving natural fathers or grandfathers. In a study done by the writer for the Christian Civic League *Record,* in only 8 percent of sex abuse cases was the natural father of the child involved.

Columnist Evelyn Sullivan, writing to grandparents in the October 13, 1991 *Muskegon* (Michigan) *Chronicle,* summarizes a study of more than 700 students at Central Missouri State University. Sullivan cites Central Missouri's Professor Gregory E. Kennedy, who found that after a divorce these students felt the role of grandparents to be "even more important" in their lives than in homes that remain intact. Most grandparents, whether or not the parents have divorced, do have regular interaction with the grandchildren, Dr. Kennedy's study found. Significantly, most students felt closer to their maternal grandparents than to their paternal grandparents. This is important to maternal grandparents since in a divorce settlement the children are nearly always placed in custody of the mother, notes columnist Sullivan.

A grandparent's contact with the grandchildren, especially with a daughter's children, can be expected to continue pretty much as before, after a divorce. The exception to this occurs when there is bitter wrangling in which the grandparent takes sides against the spouse who is not their child. In such cases it is not uncommon for a custodial mother, shamed at her parents' behavior toward her children's father, to avoid letting the grandchildren see either set of grandparents or to favor her ex-husband's parents over her own.

Godly grandparents Etta and Harry (names and certain details changed to protect family privacy), themselves the parents of a large family, have seen a daughter, the mother of four, go through divorce. The father has remarried, though he still lives in the same community and has regular visiting privileges to the children, two pre-teens and two teens. The mother, still unmarried, is employed, and she frequently dates in the evening.

So Grandma Etta is on call whenever the kids are sick (Harry still works full time). "I felt rather silly, a white-haired old granny sitting with all those young mothers," Etta remembers of one of the first times she went to a school function in place of her daughter who had chosen a party over her child's recital. But her loving interest has been rewarded with grandkids who spend much time in her home, and who are doing well in school.

The divorce has taken its toll on the grandchildren, of course, particularly in regard to their attitude toward possessions. For instance, the father bought Harry and Etta's oldest grandson a used Camaro on his sixteenth birthday, over the protests of the grandparents, though the mother did not object when her ex-husband, ordinarily a frugal man, indulged the boy. The teen wrecked the car within a week of getting his driver's license; now wiser, the father is presently requiring the son to earn his own money for his next auto.

Maxine (another pseudonym) is a paternal grandmother of three children of divorce in a state hundreds of miles from her home. Widowed, but with sufficient means to buy plane tickets, she makes twice-yearly visits to the home of her former daughter-in-law, where she is a welcome guest and a beloved grandma. She seldom visits her son, the father of her grandchildren, however, since he has moved to another state, and she simply cannot afford the extra travel expense.

Grandma Maxine finds, however, that her visits are a means to confirm in person the love she expresses in weekly letters to a teen granddaughter who gains much direction and comfort from Grandma's epistles.

I sat one afternoon in a barber's chair and watched with delighted interest the cute, blonde toddler playing on the floor. "Your granddaughter?" I asked the barber, the burly, rough-spoken, sole proprietor of this one-chair establishment.

"Yeah! Ain't she a doll?" he exclaimed, delighted at my interest. "Her mother's a tramp, though. Runs around all night," he continued.

"I'm sorry to hear that," I murmured, embarrassed at the man's frankness about his daughter's morals to a stranger.

"Her grandma 'n' I took her from the mother," the barber went on. "Grandma has to work, so I keep her here while I'm cuttin' hair. S'pose I'll hafta put her in day care when she starts gettin' inta things."

I left that barber shop wondering why a couple who seemed to have botched rearing their daughter should believe they could do better by a granddaughter.

Realistically though, in the grace of God Christian grandparents *can* make an important difference in a grandchild's life whether they are raising the child them-selves, or, as Etta and Harry, are heavily involved, or even only involved peripherally, as in Grandma Maxine's case. But the grandparent so involved must honestly, with the Lord's help, face and correct whatever circumstances in his or her own life might have con-tributed to his son or daughter's divorce.

This is not to suggest a round of self-condemnation. Parents of adult children who get into predicaments all experience such negative thinking. Rather, though we real-ize that the adult child is responsible before God and society for whatever decisions led to the divorce, since we will surely be involved as grandparents (custodial, ordinary involvement, or peripheral), we must seek to serve our grandchildren in the manner that will best bless their lives with maturity and responsibility as they grow.

Take the case of grandparents Arnold and Annie (not their real names). An independent, long-distance trucker, Arnold was away from home much of the time when Arnie Jr. was growing up. Mother Annie took Junior to church and Sunday school, and whenever Arnold was home for a weekend, he went also.

Junior, though he admired his dad, saw him as a virtual stranger. As a teen, Junior got into trouble for petty crimes and drinking. Arnold's response was to paddle him on Annie's complaint when he came home. But Junior, never disciplined by his father until he became a teen, reacted in confusion and bitterness.

The open road was Arnold's life, and he drove the best rig on the highway. He was determined to stick it out until his tractor-trailer was paid for. But frequent trades for newer models constantly pushed that magic date further off.

Junior, meanwhile, married at eighteen, then joined the Navy, leaving his pregnant bride with Annie while he did his four-year-tour of duty, seldom coming home for his leaves. Junior had met his bride in a bar; not surprisingly, she spent many of her evenings in bars after the birth of Missy, Arnold and Annie's only grandchild.

Arnold finally sold his truck and came home to stay and run a filling station. Junior's wife left two-year-old Missy with Grandma and Grandpa a month later and ran away to a street life in California. So Arnold and Annie petitioned the courts for sole custody of Missy, and they got her.

Missy, now seventeen, has no memory of her mother. Her father, remarried and raising a family in another state, is like a distant uncle. Grandma and Grandpa she views as her parents. Grandpa is now home most evenings, and he has taken an active part in the ministry of his church. Missy is secure in their love, and she is an outgoing teenager, doing well in school and regular in church, and she will probably go to college.

The change in this case was not only in Arnold's decision at last to stay home. Missy and her father, Junior, are temperamentally different as well. Arnold and Junior clashed, not only because Arnold was absent for long stretches and had failed to make friends with his son, but because they were both combative and opinionated in their dispositions. Missy, by contrast, wins Grandpa over by learning his philosophies, and, though she frequently doesn't agree with his outspoken opinions, she has learned to support him when she feels he's right and only chuckle when she disagrees. It is likely that Missy will eventually marry a man like Grandpa Arnold and make a solid marriage.

◆

*Grandfathers are especially
needed in a split-family situation,*

perhaps more than grandmothers, since children are usually with their mothers and do not suffer as much for want of adult female role modeling. Though my own family was solid and my parents' marriage was never in question, many times it was my grandfathers or an elderly uncle, for instance, who set an example for me. Grandpa Fuller, after he closed his store, expanded his woodworking shop. I can still smell the pine shavings on his floor as I did as a young teen watching him at work, proud that Grandpa's lawn furniture sprouted behind picket fences—some of which he'd also built—all across our little village. And it was the tales of long ago told by Grandpa Wiggin and Great-uncle Oscar which opened my imagination to story-telling, making it possible for me to write for children so that several of *their* stories have been retold for thousands in my Sunday school paper series and books.

Christian psychologist Dr. James Dobson warned his supporters in a June 1992 letter that without "mature, responsible men" as role models, boys without fathers often find "a surrogate family" in teen gangs, especially in the inner city. I see this as a challenge to split-family grandads to become surrogate dads to their own grandsons. If your grandson has no father at home, it is you, Grandpa, who must attend his ballgames and music recitals, take him to church, take him fishing or camping, listen to his failings and fears, dreams and triumphs. Perhaps, as in the case of a prominent Christian leader whose daughter divorced, you and Grandma may need to take that grandson into your home for a few years. That grandson, by the way, is now himself a responsible adult Christian leader!

◆

Granddaughters who are children of divorce
need strong, loving grandfathers nearby.

This is doubly so if the father has become inaccessible. And with grandparents, as with parents, the most important thing you can do for a granddaughter from a broken home is to love her grandmother. There is ample evidence that girls, for good or bad, choose husbands like the men who were their mentors and models while they were growing up.

◆

So, be there when your
granddaughter needs you.

Take her with you and Grandma on a vacation, perhaps. Give her an ear to her fears and musings, whether about things at school, a new boyfriend, or parents that misunderstand. Mothers raising children alone tend to get crotchety, simply from not having a husband to share the burden. A non-critical, non-judgmental ear from a grandparent in such a case can lift the spirits of a grandchild and ease the load of a harried mother.

◆

Go cautious on coming between that
granddaughter or grandson and the mother

or other family members whom she or he is trying to love. Let's say she complains about her mother's fiance or a grandparent on the other side. You can listen. You can sympathize with her feelings of estrangement. Often you can give mature advice. But criticize? Bite your tongue, or you may become the one who's lost his influence in that young life. There is a warning from Solomon that the person who bitterly criticizes his parents will have his influence snuffed out like a lamp in pitch darkness (see Prov. 20:20). Likewise, your influence over your grandchildren may go out like a lamp in a storm if you attack their parents or others whom they love.

The problem of involvement in your grandchild's life can become compounded when the parents remarry and the parents of the stepparent enter the picture. They may stay on the fringes or they may wish to get involved. This is understandable, especially if they are already the grandparents of the new stepparent's children. So don't force your attention. Do be available. The grandchild will gravitate to the one whom he or she prefers to spend time with.

Columnist Sullivan found it "interesting" that the majority of the 700 college students surveyed, now old enough to reflect on the consequences of their parents divorce, felt closer to their mother's parents than to their father's or to the parents of stepparents. So if you are the maternal grandparent of a child of divorce, you can expect your responsibilities to increase sharply. Are you ready?

10

Grandparents across the Miles

"You goin' t' *stay*, Grandpa?" I can still remember the urgency in my voice as I stood on the running board of Grandpa Fuller's '36 Chevy panel truck and peered into his lined face, framed with a rumpled straw hat. I knew the answer to that question before I spoke, however. The motor was still idling, and Grandma was already clambering out the other side as he reached for the gearshift to put it in reverse.

Grandpa's pleasant, "Some other time" was drowned by Mother's hurried direction to "Get off that running board and step back! Your grandfather's got a store to tend."

For my maternal grandparents, grandparenting across the miles meant a five-minute jounce over two miles of pot-holed gravel road between their place on the main road and our farm home on a crossroad. Whenever Grandma wanted to spend an afternoon with her daughter and grandchildren, Grandpa could put out a "Back in ten minutes" sign during a lull in business and expect any customer to be sitting on the steps when he returned. A man of affairs, small as they were, Grandpa got to stay only on holidays.

My maternal grandparents both lived to see all ten of their grandchildren born. Except when we older ones were in college, we were all nearby until our grandparents' deaths.

But what a change a generation has made! By the time my quiver had filled with our four youngsters, both of their grandfathers had passed on. We were 575 miles from the nearest grandma, my mother, at the birth of our youngest, and nearly 800 miles from Dot's mother. Both grandmothers could drive, but they restricted their driving trips to local jaunts. Their travels were limited to auto journeys with family members or when they went by bus, train, or plane.

My mother, who had expected to spend her days in Maine in the farmhouse two miles from her parents' home, with several grandchildren nearby, is now widowed. Instead she has settled with two unmarried daughters in Indiana, near one family of grandchildren. The others are scattered in Michigan, Wisconsin, Kentucky, and Texas, with married grandchildren in California and Kansas. And, I think, in a society where the average American family moves once every five years, Mother's situation is quite common.

Happily, for grandparents in the late twentieth century, distances are not the challenge they once were. Jack Wyrtzen recalls, for example, that "for twenty years our Bible institute in Brazil," directed by his son-in-law, "didn't even have a telephone." But now that there are grandchildren in Brazil, "I can call right into my daughter's bedroom, so we usually wake her up in the middle of the night, because of the time difference." He chuckles. Letters and express mail receive one- or two-day service nowadays. Or Grandma can step aboard a jet in New York in the forenoon and be in Los Angeles or even Honolulu in time for supper with the grandchildren.

Visiting with grandchildren, especially if the grandparents are elderly or in poor health, many times comes about when the children themselves make the trip and bring the grandchildren along. But many grandparents, relieved from employment responsibilities or in a position to take extended vacations not possible when they were younger, and perhaps with more cash to spend, are in a far better position to journey to see the grandchildren than vice-versa.

Whether both grandparents are living will affect the type of trip and the length of stay, of course. For instance, whereas a couple may plan a two-week auto tour, with weekend stops at the grandchildren's home, a widowed grandmother may take a plane, fly direct, and stay for a month.

Here are some suggested trip ideas for grandparents:

◆

Buy a light camper top
for a pickup truck.

The truck can be your second car if you are still employed. Some folks enjoy pickups anyway, and nowadays they are available with as many options as a sedan, and some of them are just as comfortable. If you buy a light, truck-mounted camper, it can be placed on skids behind your garage during the eleven months or so it won't be used. Air-adjustable shocks will permit a sedan-like ride when the truck is empty. (Caveat: Don't buy a four-wheel drive or a truck with commercial-duty suspension. Such vehicles cost more, ride hard, and generally hog gas. Unless you're going into the hinterlands in mud or snow season, a two-wheel-drive will handle a camper as handily as a four-wheeler.)

If you limit yourself to a small camper with bedroom space only, the expense will be minimal. You can travel when you feel like it, rest when you feel like it, eat in restaurants or at a rest area, and park in a rented lot at a campground with a bathhouse for a fraction of the cost of a motel. This will enable you to park at the grandchildren's for as long or as short a stay as you are welcome, then like Roy Rogers' "Tumblin' Tumbleweed," mosey on.

◆

A light
camping trailer

will give you similar advantages to a pickup camper if you already own a mid-sized or full-sized sedan adequate to pull it. For trips more than 100 miles or so, a six-cylinder vehicle is needed; eight is better. A trailer has the added advantage of your being able to unhitch and drive off, though they can be tricky to tow. But with your rolling bedroom, you can park in your children/ grandchildren's back yard for a couple of weeks in most communities—but clear it with them before you leave home! This way, you can sack in mornings until your son or son-in-law leaves for work without being a nuisance. For variety, let the grandkids camp out in your camper on Friday night while you sleep in their room. Then if the adults wish a leisurely Saturday breakfast without the kids, you won't be disturbed.

◆

Furnish a
grandparents' room

at your own expense. This will need to be cleared with your daughter/daughter-in-law and son-in-law/son, of course. You might help them purchase a new or used hide-a-bed for the family room, for instance. Or, if you'll be staying in the children's room while they camp out in the back yard, you may wish to upgrade a child's bed with a box spring and innerspring mattress to replace the link springs and foam slab designed for children. *You* will appreciate it now; the kids will appreciate it ever after.

◆

Consider buying the grandkids
a backyard tent and sleeping bags,

if your presence will overcrowd their home. Again, this should be done only after discussion with their parents.

*Buy plane, train, or bus
tickets on special offers,*

well in advance. Also, if you don't mind an auto trip on either end of the flight, trips between major cities become much more affordable, and you can avoid many layovers and plane changes. For example, when Grandma Hackney, my kids' Michigan maternal grandmother, wanted to visit her grandchildren 1,100 miles away in Maine, she found that a flight from West Michigan with two stopovers and a plane change in a strange metropolitan airport was more than she could manage. But a direct flight from Detroit was manageable and much more affordable. Her daughter drove her to Detroit (three hours), and we drove her to Maine from Boston (three hours), though the flight itself took only two hours! Two weeks later, we reversed the process. A good time was had by all—and the kids got a kick out of knowing that Grandma was getting off the plane in Detroit before we arrived home in Mid-coastal Maine!

◆

*Delight your children
overseas with a visit.*

Such trips can be surprisingly inexpensive and trouble free if you can get off-peak-traffic rates and have the advice of a seasoned international traveler to help. If your children are doing missionary service, such a trip should be cleared with their mission board, who may help you with customs and will probably furnish accommodations at a modest fee. If you have special skills useful in a third-world country, you might combine such a trip with short-term missionary service. This also must be cleared with the mission board. I'd suggest asking your pastor for advice, as a starting point.

Jim and Shirley Franks, who for years had grandchildren in Niger, West Africa, and for a while in Tokyo, have visited both sets of grandchildren in their overseas homes. Jim's experience as a globe-trotting director of Christian relief has eased setting up these visits, of course. But the Franks used these trips to supply their African grandchildren, living in a remote village where their dad is a missionary surgeon, with books and electronic educational materials their daughter can use in home-schooling the grandkids. Not surprisingly, Grandma and Grandpa Franks' home is a favorite spot to visit when the youngsters come to America.

◆

Write, write, write— write often!

The value of letters to establish and maintain long-distance grandparenting relationships is sadly neglected nowadays. And avoid photocopied, catch-all letters. These are fine for general information sent to several families at holiday time. But you should include a paragraph or two of personal greetings to each grandchild.

Nearly two thousand years ago the young church in Israel, Asia Minor, and Southern Europe was held together and built up in the faith by *letters,* known in our Bible as "epistles." Some of these were addressed to individuals, such as Timothy, Philemon, or Theophilus. Others were written to churches, groups of Christians. Paul, the greatest letter writer of all, evidently authored several—perhaps many—epistles that have not become part of the Bible and have been lost. Since God saw fit to use letters in Bible times and since then to bless so many millions of people, can he not use a letter from Grandma and Grandpa to bless your grandchildren?

And send tapes, both audio and video, if you have the means to produce them. How my own two-year-old grandson likes to play with a phone, pretending it's Grandma or Grandpa on the line! How about hearing Grandma or Grandpa—or seeing them—every time that preschooler who can't yet read letters punches a button?

❖

*Books will get to
your grandchildren*

with that special message on your heart, say Jack and Joan Wyrtzen. "Auntie—Christmas, 1947" is written in a flowing hand in a book of animal stories given me as a child, which my four children have all since enjoyed and which my grandchildren will surely enjoy (I have books which belonged to *my* grandparents!). A mind prepared early with good literature (check with your grandkids' mothers to see if they're actually being read) from childhood is more readily receptive to books on spiritual topics both then and later on.

◆

*Grandma, plan your
trip with care.*

A lot of grandmothers travel by auto, and this can be either happy or hair-raising, depending on your preparedness. I suggest you have a towing and road service provision with wide acceptance on your auto insurance policy or else join an auto club. Have basic maintenance done on your auto two to three weeks beforehand. This will allow time to work out bugs caused by mechanics' mistakes. For instance, one lady left for an extended trip the day after she'd had a cruise control installed. She had to call a tow truck the first day out because of a kink in a vacuum hose which made the car inoperable.

◆

*Have a friend who understands
autos check everything out*

because even the most competent service garage will overlook small details which could leave you stranded. While helping my grandchildren, I recently borrowed my mother's station wagon for a trip of several hundred miles. Mother is a great-grandmother, and she ordinarily has her car meticulously serviced. So everything *looked* okay, but I was in a hurry.

A nearly new tire blew late at night on a busy expressway. So Grandpa (myself) pulled the spare from Great-grandma's wagon and attempted to change the wheel. But the lug nuts were rusty, and the factory-equipment wrench was inadequate to remove the wheel. Moral: have a friend grease those wheel lugs yearly (tire shops almost never do this), and buy yourself a nice, big, star-type universal wheel wrench. Even if you can't change a tire yourself, you need adequate tools so someone else can, and the wrench supplied with your car is very possibly too flimsy.

◆

*Trip planning
services can help,*

but planners often overlook road construction. Friends of ours lost two hours coming across the Virginia Blue Ridge because their planning service relied on outdated maps. A phone call to us at their destination would have prevented this.

◆

*Plan your physical check-ups
about a month before your trip.*

If you need dental work or new glasses, you'll want your own doctor to do the work. And, like auto repairs, dental and ocular work often need adjusting after a week or so.

◆

*Don't carry more cash than
you'll need to get there.*

Check with your son or daughter in advance, and be sure they can cash a personal check for you if you bank with a credit union that's not tied into a nationwide money-machine network, such as Cirrus. You can arrange for direct deposit of Social Security checks so you don't need to be home to collect them.

◆

*It's unwise to start a
journey requiring night driving*

if you're past seventy. Older folks often suffer from night blindness, and even with glasses corrected to 20/20 for daylight hours, they can find themselves positively helpless after dark, especially in rain, fog, or swirling snow. And if you're traveling far on strange roads, consider investing in a portable CB radio, to call police or alert a passing truck driver that you need help. And by all means, carry a telephone credit card (available free from your phone company) and a list of all phone numbers you'll need at your destination(s) and back home.

◆

*Get all prescriptions filled
before you leave home,*

and carry sufficient medicines with you to last the trip. Running out of allergy medicine can make your trip miserable; running short of heart medicine could be life threatening. If you're diabetic, carry an adequate supply of insulin and syringes whenever traveling across state lines since some states require a prescription for them.

◆

*Grandmas, and Grandpas
too, will want to carry small gifts*

for the younger grandchildren. Make these unique to your state or region, and they'll be treasured forever, even by children with no sense of geography. I learned as a child that Boston must be a wonderful place. Though Grandma Wiggin lived right in our house, her sisters—my great aunts—came from Boston each summer, and the trinkets from their bags, though seldom for children, seemed as exotic as if St. Nick himself had opened his pack on our kitchen table.

*Put the grandkids and
their parents first,*

and you'll all have a happy visit. I recommend visiting
when the kids are out of school, so you can take them to
the zoo or other nearby recreation area. But it's often
unwise to plan your visit during their father's (your son
or son-in-law's) vacation from work, except for holidays. Four adults, plus kids, in one household for a week
or two often get on each other's nerves, though if Dad is
working he will enjoy having you around evenings. You
may even wish to take each other out for supper.

If your vacation coincides with your grandchildren's
parents', and you decide to follow them to their lakeside
cottage in Minnesota, a short visit of a day and a night
might be in order. Then leave! At the least, rent your
own cabin. Dads, especially, covet vacation time to
spend alone with their wife and kids.

◆

*There are exceptions
to this, of course.*

Many families plan stay-at-home vacations because
they *want* the grandparents around. A full round of family activities, planned and unplanned, is enjoyed by all.
The men may work together rebuilding a car or go golf-

ing. The women spend their time in joint activities. Several days are dedicated to the kids. Mature discretion and honest discussion beforehand should determine which approach to take.

◆

The basic rule in
long-distance grandparenting,

then is the "law of Christ" (see Gal. 6:2; Luke 10:25-27): to love one's neighbor—grandchild, or that grandchild's parents, as yourself. This requires planning, with their needs uppermost. Put aside the all-too-common concept of purposely using family as free lodging along a larger trip—this may occur, but what is your motive? Rather, what can *you* give them of yourself? That's the key!

11

When Your Grandchild's Ears
Fall Off

My birthday cake for Mother was a crashing disaster. Not only was it heavy and the layers soggy in the middle, but when I tried to frost it, chunks the size of quarters peeled off and mixed with the frosting.

Grandma's handwritten recipe book listed only ingredients. Other directions this venerable master cook kept in her head. And so it was that I ventured into the room where Grandma was entertaining to ask her explanation of a routine step. I'm sure *her* answer was adequate and understandable. But advice was hurled at me by a supercilious bevy of ladies whose baking abilities evidently exceeded their communication skills.

At that moment, my ears fell off. I retreated miserably to the kitchen to mix a cake better suited for Halloween!

"That child didn't hear a thing I said!" I'm sure every grandparent has said this at least once. Grandma's friends would surely have said that had they been on hand when my cake was cut. To this day, I don't know what went wrong with the cake.

Grandparents and grandchildren fail to communicate for a variety of reasons. Often we blame inattention, TV, or childish rudeness. And these are problems often enough. But a careful physician will seek to eliminate all known causes before he makes a diagnosis requiring radical surgery. If your grandchild, be he eight or eighteen, is afflicted with dropoffsey of the audio orifices, check all problems before fixing blame. Here are several problems and suggested cures for falling ears.

◆

Commands and instructions instead of conversation

will tune a child out. Forgetting the magic "please" will tell a child that he's of less worth than an adult as quickly as anything. You say, "Do this, Johnny"; or, "Run next door and ask to borrow a screwdriver." But, unless there is loving reciprocity and thoughtful consideration with the request, these demands will quickly reduce your grandchild to one of the Old Lady in the Shoe's "many children." Asking a grandchild to be your "go-for" is one thing. Forgetting to be courteous to him as an individual is quite another. If you've given a child permission to watch a TV show, for example, is it thoughtful to interrupt the most exciting episode to ask him to run an errand?

Children are deaf
to nostalgia.

Many adults don't have a clue on this one, and they persist in being fooled for years because once upon a time there was a good little child who heard *every* word of your nostalgic tale. And the kid was interested. Nice kid? Or did your story hook that child with a non-nostalgic point of interest which you did not even recognize?

Here's a case in point: When I was a kid, we had a Jersey bull, old Turk. He had brown eyes, crumpled horns, and a brass ring in his nose. His coat was as ashen as death itself. Turk was the Minotaur reincarnated.

Then one evening Grandpa told me the ox story. As a boy, he'd been sent by his father one December day onto the frozen bog below our farm to fetch an ox-drawn pung-load of swale grass, cut and cocked in July. But the oxen broke through the crust and climbed in terror onto the mound of hay. Grandpa, a teen at the time, shouldered the yoke and left the dumb, trembling brutes for the night. Next morning, he found them at the barn door, lowing for their breakfast.

Grandpa loved nostalgia. But having never lived in the past, I had no appreciation for it. It took a gigantic leap of faith, in fact, to imagine my old grandfather carrying a yoke nearly a mile on his shoulder.

And I had never seen an ox. But Grandpa explained they were "something like bulls, but gentler." I loved animals, and fierce ol' Turk I understood. So I found it amusing to imagine creatures "something like" his ilk cowering on a snow-covered mound of hay. I was interested in the story for the story's sake.

I recall my fascination with learning how to make a wooden whistle from a green willow shoot with bark that could be slipped off. My grandfather's cleverness in making this simple toy amazed and delighted me. Only after the whistle was completed did I learn that "every boy in school had one of these" in the 1870s.

Having never lived in the past, children have no interest in nostalgia. But they are interested in *new* experiences—not new to the world, necessarily, but new to *their* experience. Much of your past as a grandparent *is* new to your grandchildren, and it can be related interestingly, if given the right perspective. For instance, besides animals, children like humor and adventure.

◆

Grandparents must
respect the present,

and they must be glad listeners to their grandchildren's reports of things that impress *them.* Fifteen-year-old Brad is impressed with Corvettes. Me, I'd much rather tour a gravel country lane in a '32 Chevy roadster, but to Brad, it's just an old car.

Few youth can appreciate nostalgia until they are older teens. Your "I remember" story of a hard-fought battle driving the Nazis out of France may interest pre-teens. But your thrill at riding in a victory parade afterward, the second car back from General Eisenhower ("Who was he?!") may lose them.

◆

Are you interested in your grandchild's "little things?"

Can you honestly listen to a fourteen-year-old's contemporary Christian song and appreciate the lyrics with him even if you don't care for the arrangement? Or, little Johnny has dug up a rusted, nondescript metal object in your garden: "What's this, Grandma?" Do you impatiently direct him to the garbage can? Or can you share the interest of your budding archaeologist and help him scrape it clean with an old kitchen knife, cementing a bond with Johnny which will be rewarded with many happy conversations?

◆

Do you hear, really,

what little Tammy, age five, is trying to say? "I think there's a monster in the closet," she whines. You may say, "There's no monsters in this house. Go back to sleep, dear." Or do you help her find the things that go bump in the night?

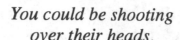

*You could be shooting
over their heads.*

For instance, most kids under fifteen (and a lot of adults, as well!) simply lack the knowledge of electrical circuits to understand why opening a window when one is hot isn't as efficient a means of cooling a room as lowering the thermostat. If you've got a twelve-year-old grandson with a mind for science, and he sincerely wants to know, explain how a thermostat works. Any child can understand, however, that when a window is opened in wintertime, heat, which costs money to produce, rushes outdoors. But don't push. Many things a child has to take on faith—it's true because Grandpa says so.

Can you tell a child how to tie a shoelace? I can't; I don't know how myself. But I can tie my laces with my eyes shut. And I can *show* a child how to tie his shoe! Here's a clue to many conversations with children that impatient adults should learn. Often a picture, a demonstration, an illustration will work. Facts are dull and dreary without sufficient points of reference to understand them.

◆

*Lying is a
sure turn-off.*

When little Johnny is four he may believe Grandpa's story about the "dangerous wild bull" in the tumbledown barn behind the house, not knowing it was concocted to keep him out. At six, Johnny has learned better—and he's learned not to trust Grandpa. So his ears fall off whenever Grandpa speaks.

Tall tales for comic effect—the Paul Bunyan variety—may be okay if they're understood to be fantasy. But bizarre yarns which are designed principally to impress kids with one's knowledge of the unusual soon wear thin, especially when told first-person, and your grandchild has already heard it elsewhere.

◆

Ask their advice.

They'll listen to this one every time. Grandma's car won't start, so before she calls the garage, she calls on grandson Eddie, fifteen. She's delighted to learn that Eddie's dad had the same problem, and Eddie knows what to do. And Eddie, intoxicated by Grandma's trust in him, suddenly becomes a listener *and* a talker.

◆

Eavesdrop without snooping.

As a frequent substitute teacher in school classrooms, I've learned to tune my ears to bits of conversation by teens who may—or may not—have their work done. Never, ever peek into a child's diary or listen on another line to a private phone conversation, of course. But when your teen grandkids are chatting over the ping-pong table or commenting on the Sunday sermon, for instance, you may gain valuable insights into their thought processes by listening in the shadows. Or, listen when you drive with teens. Many kids become motormouths while motoring along, and via their mouths you learn what's going on inside their heads and hearts.

◆

With teens, still
water may run deep.

In trying to deal with teen grandchildren on a kid's level, you may have inadvertently ignored their ability to grasp, though imperfectly, weighty concepts of the adult world. Both Einstein and Edison were marked as slow learners by teachers who didn't make the effort to tune in to their thoughts, for example.

Some teens seem interested only in food, clothes, sports, cars, movies, or the other sex, to be sure. But teens can also be concerned about how to curb runaway welfare costs, the Arab-Israeli conflict, Mozart, starvation in Somalia, or evangelism in Eastern Europe. Try them on these, or similar topics. You might find a young intellectual or a youth with great spiritual concerns beneath that glum demeanor!

◆

Be
understanding.

Grandparents, even those who relate readily to younger children may find themselves dismayed by teens. Here's where the transition from parent to grandparent can be trying, especially if it's been a few years since you had teens of your own.

Twelve-year-old Tabitha is your five-foot-two, blue-eyed darling. She's flat-chested and athletic, but today she's in the doldrums over having loved and lost. *You* see Tabitha on the parallel bars demonstrating her skill at gymnastics, or playing a piano solo, pert, with a black satin bow in her ash-blonde hair at a Sunday evening church concert. *She* sees herself as Cinderella, whose prince has just found another princess!

◆

She'll get
over it,

you ponder. But how can you convey this to her gently and compassionately without destroying communication? To dismiss her feelings of dismay as a silly crush would only bring a hurt, perhaps angry, response: "Grandma, you couldn't understand!"

◆

Do you understand, really?

At twelve, Tabitha is probably capable of the same range of affections and emotions (romance, passionate sexual desire, to name a couple) as an adult female. But she lacks the understanding of her emotions that you have or her mother has.

"Bear ye one another's burdens, and so fulfill the law of Christ" (Gal. 6:2). To love one another is a truth that underscores what Grandma's attitude ought to be toward your Tabitha or another teen grandchild. Have you forgotten your own heartrending first breakup with a boyfriend or fiance, Grandma? After your burden-bearing, woman-to-woman empathizing *(not* woman-to-girl!), you may wish to get Grandpa involved, especially if Tabitha's dad is not living in the home. Grandpa could take her out to dinner while Grandma stays home. He may get her to open up by telling her about *his* own experiences.

I recall sitting on a bench beside the Evangeline Chapel in a park in Grand Pre, Nova Scotia and exchanging words of anguish with the young woman of my dreams many years ago. Next morning, my last glimpse of this walnut-haired, brown-eyed Canadian lass from Acadia was the swish of her salmon-pink skirt as she disappeared through the imposing double doors of the newspaper office where she worked as a typesetter. And I was left facing a solitary twelve-hour drive in my ancient chariot to get home. Perhaps some day I'll tell *that* story (every word of it is true!) to one of my granddaughters in love!

12

Who's That Boy with the Pimples?

Several teens from my growing-up years come to mind as I write this. One we called "Beanpole" was skinny and he stood six-foot-three by his fourteenth birthday. "How's the weather up there?" or, "Didn't know they piled it that high," were the smirking greetings the guys met Beanpole with. Beanpole had pimples, and he could often be found doctoring his face in front of a mirror, hunched over the wash basin to get low enough to see his forehead.

Beanpole left our sparsely settled rural community to disappear into a big-city jungle right after high school. Bitter, hurt by childhood schoolmates, Beanpole has not been seen in our town in forty years, not even for his mother's funeral.

"Bob" is any of half a dozen guys I knew. He was of medium build, five-foot-ten-and-a-half, which took him fifteen and a half years to achieve. No zits ever scarred his boyish grin, nor did blackheads ever trouble him. If they did, he got rid of them at home before school.

Bob is today successful, respected, and loved by family and friends in the community in which he grew up.

◆

Odd things happen to kids at twelve or so which can mark them for life, strange things that grandparents who do not have at least monthly contact with their grandchildren may find surprising, even confusing.

We tend to measure our grandchildren against our own childhood and the childhoods of our children. We may not have raised a Beanpole. All of our own kids may have been Bobs. But as the gene pool broadens with each generation, the possibilities likewise enlarge. And we're surprised with a grandchild who's different, especially if we haven't seen him or her since they were small. Watch it, though. "You're taller'n your dad, already"; or, "My, how you're filling out," may bring shame instead of pride, accentuating Eddie or Susie's secret belief that they were mistakenly placed here from another planet.

In reality, each teen grandchild represents a different piece of the mosaic we accept as normal, a piece which perhaps we have not had experience with.

Bob was normal.

Beanpole was normal, also. But neither he nor his schoolmates could accept this. I suspect his family did not believe him normal, either.

Growth spurts, like slow growth, are normal. Young people, age twelve to about fifteen, may suffer excruciating concerns about their normality or lack thereof. Teens, especially younger teens, are extremely peer conscious, and they tend to measure the normalcy of others (including their parents and grandparents!) by the opinions and standards of their peers. A fourteen-year-old, for instance, may not think it's normal for granddads to wear hats. And if his granddad, who's bald and doesn't want to burn, insists on wearing a brimmed hat to a soccer game and looking like Calvin Coolidge, he'd better wear it straight, *at least!* More than one fedora-adorned grandfather has had a jauntily cocked felt or straw shade straightened by an indignant grandson or granddaughter at the door. "Grandpa, you look like some kind of ethnic freak with it on *that* way," is the stock young teen explanation.

The seventh grade can mark a confusing time of changes for the average twelve- or thirteen-year-old, and for some few, these changes can be frightening, even traumatic. Your grandchild, used to a self-contained school classroom in his K-6 years, with perhaps an outside teacher for music or art, now changes rooms and teachers every hour. Friends he's hung onto during his elementary years may disappear into the jungle that is junior high, not to reappear again until bus time.

He or she plunges into sexual maturation, which in our culture can have its cruel aspects. Several times a week students disrobe to change for gym and shower—usually in groups—and stages in sexual development become apparent, sometimes painfully so, as insecure bullies make crude remarks about bodily hair, or the lack thereof, or the size of bosoms or private parts. Woe be to the smooth-skinned, plump boy with sagging breasts and childlike genitals. And flat-chested, athletic Twiggys, or girls with earlier than average breast development, can be tormented by insecure but clever-tongued girls who may be jealous.

I've noticed a new sexual phenomenon in school classrooms and corridors which is largely a product of the 1990s. Remember when references to the privates was limited to boys-only or girls-only sessions? Though remarks then were often vulgar, at least decency between the sexes was preserved. Today's youth, as a result of the breakdown of their parents' marriages and urged along by frankly sexual TV shows, teen magazines, R and PG-13 movies, and mixed-sex sex-ed sessions, have exchanged the old, familiar four-letter words for privates for the clinical terms for genitals. Though frankness in proper context is healthy, normal fascination with sexuality passes the limits of decency when reference to penises and vaginas, along with the f-word, become the vocabulary of light, mixed-sex chatter in the back row during so-called study hall.

A Florida public school teacher, writing in "Ann Landers" in July 1992, complains of conditions in her school where "fights, thefts, drug sales, and weapons" have become a constant problem. "Threats and filthy language" in the corridors are regular occurrences, and disruptions by "lewd comments, raucous laughter, and loud arguments with teachers" make education all but impossible. This report was balanced out by a letter from a teacher in Dayton who found even inner-city students to be "well mannered and respectful" and gladly accepting a dress code of the type many other schools find unenforceable.

As a substitute teacher on call in two West Michigan counties, both elementary and secondary, I can take you to schools within ten miles of each other where either the Florida or Dayton patterns are the norm. It takes a firm, well-balanced staff of administrators and teachers in cooperation with wide-awake parents to run a school these days without chaos. Your grandchildren may be enrolled in either kind of school.

◆

Today's young teen grandchild
may be thrust from innocence into
the context of competitive sexuality.

This includes easy banter from both boys and girls about sexual experiences at age thirteen. Today's teen is the second generation of American youth to attend the sprawling consolidated schools instituted right after the grandparents of today finished high school. So, a teen today is faced with a mind-boggling assortment of attitudes, opinions, and behaviors, crowding in with relentless insistence that he sample this, look at that, hear this story, learn another thing in corridor, restroom, and classroom that may contradict or compromise the values of his home or church, or even of the relatively supportive environment of the elementary school. These cry out for him to question all old authority and to transfer his loyalty to a new authority—the school and the peer group. And this comes on with a rush in the context of his or her wonderfully developing new appetites.

Teens universally suffer the illusion that sexuality is the exclusive domain of folks under thirty, who magically discovered it as a historical first. If Columbus was surprised to discover Indians in the New World, young teens are incredulous when told by parents or grandparents that intense, powerful sexual appetites have been around since Adam marveled at the new twists and curves the Lord had given his rib while he slept. This illusion is part of a natural, universally acknowledged God-given moral agency which insists that sex should be a private joy to be shared between two people in the context of: a. Virginity until marriage; and, b. exclusiveness during marriage. Elisabeth Elliot, for example, reports in *The Savage My Kinsman,* that pagan Auca Indians, who wore little or no clothing, vigorously protected the privacy of their sexuality, and adulterers could be speared to death.

What too often happens in American culture, I believe, is that sexual loyalty and privacy, which God intended to be single-spousal-directed, becomes peer directed. Teens share amongst themselves—snickering, bragging, giggling; or at times intensely serious—thoughts, appetites, and tragically often, actions, which should be saved for a private encounter with a lifelong helpmeet. For example, I recently overheard a snickering teen girl ask a boy, in a stage whisper intended for the vicarious pleasure of classmates around them—but not for the teacher's ears—if he was having regular sex with his girlfriend.

With such shared (debauched) sexual experience (vicarious or real) often comes a wall of exclusiveness and secrecy which draws on the emotions God intended to make marriage an exclusive, no-one-else's business relationship. Instead, this exclusiveness is transferred to the peerage of teens, and even youth from Christian homes who may not share these experiences are often drawn into the net.

All too often this exclusiveness shuts parents, grandparents, and pastors outside the youth's circle of privacy. What can ensue is a game lasting three, five, or even seven years in which children try to keep adults out of their private worlds, and parents and grandparents work out a truce with the teens by which both can function with a modicum of civility.

The Beanpoles with the pimples are pretty much left out of this bittersweet society. This can happen to either sex, of course, but girls, with greater social skills than guys, often manage to build bridges with other girls, with younger kids, or even find satisfaction in tending others' babies. And a girl's social facility is no doubt an important reason why fewer girls than guys engage in premarital sex.

Being left out, however, while it can cause a teen to turn on himself in lowered self-esteem, may actually have a positive side. Joseph, for instance, had been forcibly ejected from the society of his brothers, one of whom—Judah—had unveiled his low moral principles by visiting a supposed prostitute (see Gen. 37:26-27; 38:15-16). Yet solitary Joseph, a slave in a strange land, rose to be second in command in the state in early adulthood!

◆

Most youth feel alone
part or much of the time.

I believe that's the natural, normal order of things. Adam was "alone" for a time after his creation, for example (see Gen. 2:18).

Teens find themselves alone, not so much because they're in a growth spurt which may make them seem like a Frankensteinian freak to their peers, but because they have left the garden of childhood with its vine-hung walls of parental affection, never to return.

When I was a young teen I was an avid reader of Zane Grey westerns. I loved these stories—the man in the saddle, the faithful horse, the marshal who mistook him for a wanted rustler, nights under the stars with the howl of coyotes and the hoot of owls as companions. I sensed my aloneness, yet I couldn't put a finger on it. But here was a man I could relate to (Grey died the year I was born!) because, though from an earlier generation, he knew how to express being alone as a thrill, a challenge.

My son Brad, at fifteen, has recently discovered westerns, and the other day I left him at the library to search for the latest volumes of Louis L'Amour. "While you're at it, pick up a Zane Grey title," I gently proposed.

"Aw, Dad, that's *old* stuff. You read that when you were a kid."

"Yes," I chuckled. "So did your grandfather. I got hooked on Grey by reading *his* old books."

Brad came home with two L'Amour and a moldy copy of Grey. "Hey, Dad," he exclaimed the next day, "this guy's pretty good. In some ways I like Zane Grey better'n Louis L'Amour!"

Zane Grey was onto a timeless need of youth. Young Jacob, alone, wrestled with God under the stars to become Israel, God's prince (see Gen. 32:24-28). Samuel, separated from his parents, alone with God in his room, was called to be the last and greatest judge of Israel (see 1 Sam. 1:24; 3:10, 19-21). Christ prayed alone at Gethsemane (see Matt. 26:36-46).

Your grandson or granddaughter, whether outwardly the smooth, fit-with-the-crowd Bob, or the awkward, gangly, Beanpole, whether guy or girl, has a felt loneliness which he or she is searching to fill. Your task is to direct that search with living support, compassion, and kindness.

◆

*For a teen troubled by the vicissitudes
of growing up, grandparents often
can offer help that parents cannot.*

Having the advantage of a third generation of maturity, and perhaps more importantly, being in a better position to take a dispassionate look at a grandchild's problems, a grandparent can soothe, console, and win confidences whereas a parent might tend to alienate.

Judy (name changed), a young teen whose parents were divorced, was often a guest in our home when I was in college. Judy lived for a time with her grandparents, but she sometimes came to my father, a man of recognized Christian maturity, with her troubles. A Christian teen, Judy very much wanted a father to talk with, and my dad, with seven kids of his own, would lend her his ears from time to time. I'm sure she worked her way through numbers of problems just by having a sympathetic male listener to help her build her self-esteem.

Author Maureen Rank, writing in *Dealing With the Dad of Your Past* (Bethany, 1990), cites a study by psychologist Dr. Daniel Trobisch. In a chapter entitled, "The Father-God Connection," Rank summarizes Trobisch that *"every woman* (italics hers) in his study saw God with the same characteristics she observed in her father." Rank concludes that girls, especially, need fathers in order to develop self-esteem and learn to love God.

Secular studies on the influence of the home on youth generally either lump both parents together or focus on the effect of the absent mother who is away at work. Cliches such as "The hand that rocks the cradle rules the world" solidify the thinking of those who revere motherhood to the exclusion of fatherhood.

But Abraham Lincoln's famous, "All that I am and ever hope to be I owe to my angel mother" has basis in fact: as girls need fathers, so boys need mothers. Adult males normally find the confirmation of their manhood in their relationship with a loving wife. But in adolescence, boys develop, through relationships with their mothers or another significant adult female such as a grandmother, confidence to court a girl worthy of their charms, courage to keep at it in college or business pursuits when others are quitting.

Though your children may not be divorced, all the same, realistically, Mom and Dad cannot always meet the needs of your teen grandson or granddaughter when they need them to. Here's where God has put Grandma in the gap to furnish the cheering squad for Grandson Eddie while playing role model for Granddaughter Susie; and Grandpa can furnish male counsel for Susie while playing role model for Eddie.

Psychiatrist Michael P. Nichols, author of *No Place to Hide* (Fireside), points out that parents, and by inference, grandparents, anxious to help teens, may alienate them by criticizing the *child* rather than correcting the wrongful *behavior.* Questions such as, "Are you really going to wear that to school?" tell a teen that what he or she "is doing is disgusting, stupid, intolerable," says Dr. Nichols.

Dealing with kids' clothes can be a delicate proposition because clothes are an extension of the personality, the very soul. Grandchildren are hurt, not because their body shape isn't average, hence "normal," or because their complexion doesn't match the silken skin of a cover model. They are hurt because others *they consider important* have taken facts about their bodies and clothing, extensions of their souls, and ground their souls into the dirt by unthinking comments.

Let's say fifteen-year-old Eddie or Susie is spending a week at Grandma's House during the school year since their parents must travel on business. Your grandchild arrived Sunday evening in fresh Sunday clothes (unlike eight year olds, teens *can* stay neat all day!). Monday morning after a shower which you fear could challenge Niagara, he/she arrives for breakfast dressed for school. The knees are out of his/her jeans. His/her loafers are worn without socks, and he/she wears a tee shirt with "Underachiever and Proud of It" in three-inch-high letters. Do you, shocked, scold? Or do you wait until your daughter phones from the hotel that evening, then query her about her scion's "styles?"

Let's say you choose the second course. When Eddie's/Susie's mother calls, her only complaint is that he/she wore no socks with those unwashable leather shoes!

That evening, after gently telling Susie why she's expected to wear socks, she remarks, "Grandma, Dad really gets a kick out of my tee shirt. He says as long as I'm getting A's in chemistry and German he doesn't care what I wear, just so it's decent." You were rewarded for holding your tongue that morning by having Susie let you into a family joke. Susie appreciates your concern, and she has not been put down by what could seem to her an attack on her individuality.

I recall a gentleman who wore a wig which so obviously was not his hair that it could be spotted across a large auditorium. He wore expensive suits and drove late-model luxury cars all the years I knew him. But not once did I question the guy's taste in toupees by suggesting that he toss his el-cheapo into file thirteen and buy a fitted hairpiece, which he could certainly afford to do. That's what mirrors are for.

As grandparents, we desire to help usher our Eddies and Susies across the threshold of adulthood. We can best do this when we realize that those youth, who much of the time are carefree and happy, are also suffering through the most trying years of life, from puberty to young maturity. We gently criticize their behavior when we must. We set guidelines and expectations when they're entrusted to our care. Even as we wouldn't question another adult's toupee or hairdo, we avoid personal remarks about our emerging-adult teens whose souls may have been torn and trampled already in the school gantlet or by conflicts at home.

But most of all, we support, we listen, we pray. And we love.

13

Grandparents Bearing Gifts

My kids' maternal grandmother has seven dozen descendants spread over four generations, for which she must remember birthdays, anniversaries, baby showers, graduation parties, and Christmas. By contrast, their paternal grandmother has a paltry two and a half dozen descendants over three generations, though hers are spread throughout a wider radius of states. Neither grandfather is living and neither grandmother is employed, so both grandmothers must make their gift selections from limited incomes.

Things were simpler when I was a child. We had four grandparents, and my maternal grandfather was employed. Each set of grandparents had a rounded dozen grandkids, but great-grandchildren, though eventually numerous, for the most part waited until the elders had passed on before being born. In common with my children's generation—and my grandchildren's— neither I nor my wife had grandparents who could afford to be heavy spenders at gift-giving times.

Communication is a powerful emollient to pour on the sometimes-troubled waters of misunderstood family relationships, especially when it comes to money spent on gifts for the grandchildren. Cross-cultural and cross-social marriages can lead to hurts that boil up like acne at gift-giving time. For starters, you will need to meet your grandchildren's other set of grandparents on several informal occasions soon after your children's wedding, either by inviting them to your home—to which they'll no doubt reciprocate—or to a modest restaurant where both couples will be comfortable.

It's tragically common for young couples with small children to isolate themselves from the grandparents, even to returning gifts sent for the grandchildren, especially where one spouse was reared to riches and the other grew up in a home of more modest means. Pride over an ambition to make it without the aid of wealthy relatives may boil over into resentment when expensive presents are given the children at Christmastime, whereas the other grandparents can afford only bargain-basement specials. This pride may bring on an emotional myopia which wrongly imagines the generosity of the wealthier grandparents to be an attempt to buy love.

So, here's where befriending those other grandparents early in the relationship, especially when there's an economic or cultural gulf to span, can provide first, insight into understanding the mind of your new daughter/son-in-law, and finally, a bridge into their hearts.

But be sure it's not *your* pride that's been wounded. Did you really expect a grandchild of eight to take better care of the L.L. Bean shirt you bought him than if it came from K-Mart, for instance?

◆

Wealth intimidates a lot of grandparents
who've never had much for earthly possessions.
And poverty may frighten some rich,
especially if they were born to wealth.

I grew up poor, and I still am, but as a journalist I've learned some interesting things about accepting and being accepted. A multi-millionaire once took me out to lunch. I had a sixty-cent fish sandwich and a Coke. Her meal was only slightly more expensive. We were both satisfied, and neither of us was embarrassed. Weeks before Dan Quayle was elected to the vice presidency, his parents, Jim and Corrine Quayle, were my guests for breakfast at a small roadside restaurant in Michigan. Both were born to wealth, but they are common folks and easy to chat with. And I found that we shared spiritual values in common, too.

The comic-strip caricatures of the rich surrounded by servants, or of the poor living in squalor, is made of about equal parts of myth and anachronism! Grandparents should not let silly fears of such imagined barriers prevent them from making friends with their grandchildren's other grandparents.

It is important to remember when buying gifts for the grandchildren that it's ordinarily not important what the other grandparents, wealthier or poorer, are buying. Clear it with the parents to avoid duplications and inappropriate presents, of course. But if one grandma who owns a controlling interest in an industrial plant buys Johnny a $400 remote-controlled car, and you send him peanut-butter fudge gift-wrapped in a fancy can—saved from a Christmas past—well, so what? He'll appreciate both, probably equally, for few eight-year-olds can fathom the worth of a battery-operated plastic auto in dollars versus the goodness of homemade fudge anyway.

The apostle Paul's teaching about the Lord's Supper (Eucharist, Communion), that sacred celebration of God's greatest gift, eternal life through the broken body and shed blood of Christ, is prefaced with some reminders about our human tendency to celebrate even Christian occasions selfishly and pridefully. Each Corinthian Christian, rather than eat at home, was going ahead with his own lunch in the company of those met to celebrate the Lord's Supper. One family would pig out, let's say, on pastrami, Swiss, and sauerkraut on rye, while another had only the first-century equivalent of soda crackers and processed cheese (see 1 Cor. 11:20-22).

Christmas in our day is the celebration when Christians and others in American Christendom sometimes vie with one another for the most attention-getting festivities. It is one thing to enjoy a tradition, such as a twelve-foot tree touching the cathedral ceiling of your family room under which the grandchildren can share a joyous occasion. It is quite another to attempt to buy love or attention with expensive gifts. Be sure, however, that you're not pridefully mistaking another's expensive celebration, to which you have been invited, as an attempt to show off.

Old Fort Wayne, a replica of the eighteenth century log fort and trading post which once stood where downtown Fort Wayne, Indiana has risen, has an annual reenactment of the various ethnic colonial Christmases celebrated there in the years when this city was a wilderness outpost just before, and for some years after, the Revolutionary War. With my children and their grandmother, I visited this festival several years ago. Each nationality had its distinct Christmas—as I recall only the Germans had a tree, a *tannenbaum*. But gift giving then was pretty much limited to small, keepsake-type items for the children.

◆

*Genuine giving must
flow out of true* love—*not the mushy variety that
says, "I just want to smother you with kisses."*

Rather, it must be *agape* love, the love that always puts that grandchild's best interests first. This is the love of God who gave us His "only begotten Son" (John 3:16); whose "gift is . . . eternal life" forever with Him (Rom. 6:23).

Gift-giving grandparents tend to have either a surplus of time or a surplus of cash; seldom both. Whereas retired grandparents living on fixed incomes usually have time on their hands to make things or to learn a craft which they may not have achieved when younger, grandparents who are still employed and whose families have grown can often afford to buy relatively expensive gifts for grandchildren.

Some grandparents, having more cash than "shop 'til you drop" stamina, may simply get the kids' sizes and order needed clothing from an L.L. Bean or J.C. Penney's catalog, depending on their budget.

Or, a grandmother with limited means and a large tribe can make a baked gift, one for a family. Personally, I prefer fruitcake. But, along with spats, bell-bottomed trousers, and accordion music, fruitcakes are held in disdain by a generation jaded by pizza and potato chips. So check whether they ate (with relish!) last year's gift before baking another. Cookies, sweet rolls, or another type of cake might be more acceptable. And packaging can be as simple as cardboard, aluminum foil, and cellophane tape.

Grandmothers with sewing machines, knitting needles, crochet hooks, or grandfathers with woodworking tools, can whip up an endless variety of handmade gifts, many destined to become family heirlooms, for minimal expense. A visit to a well-stocked supermarket magazine rack will reveal perhaps a dozen "country" magazines, craft magazines, or woodshop journals. These are filled with designs for making stuffed dolls, quilts, cushions, wooden toys, lawn or bedroom furniture, clock cases, bookcases, knick-knacks and knick-knack shelves, embroidery, stencil work, reusable Christmas wreaths, rugs, or baked goods.

My dear old Aunt Gladys had no children of her own, though she ministered to more than a thousand of others' during forty-some years as a teacher. The same age as my maternal grandmother, she once told me she thought of my father as the son she never had. And she lived to play grandmother to several of Dad's grandchildren, using turn-of-the-century patterns to make afghans for weddings and for baby showers and mittens for little hands. Some of her handiwork is now tucked away in Grandma Wiggin's cedar chest for future generations to enjoy.

Books ought to be at the head of a grandparent's shopping list, and as with most other gifts for grandchildren, consult the parents to determine the child's reading level, interests, and to avoid duplication. Visit a Christian bookstore well in advance of your shopping spree, and browse the children's, juvenile, and adult fiction sections. "Teen" fiction tends to be aimed at pre- or young teens (age ten to fourteen), so if you've got a grandchild fifteen or older, he or she will probably prefer a selection from the adult section. Some books, such as C.S. Lewis' and J.R.R. Tolkien's allegorical fantasies, appeal to pre-teen through adult, however.

Many Christian publishing houses which advertise in Christian magazines offer catalogs with a wide selection of Christian books for Christmas, birthday, or graduation giving from various sources, as well as listing their own publications.

◆

Some grandparents like to add to collections their grandchildren are building, whether dolls, stuffed animals, or baseball caps.

These can be purchased as they become available, often on vacation trips. Or, in the case of dolls or Teddy bears, Grandma may wish to make one with her own name sewn into it as a reminder to Granddaughter to pass it on as an heirloom to her own granddaughter. And Grandpa may wish to complement a doll collection by building Granddaughter a fine doll house.

Gifts of clothing are usually appreciated, and if Grandma is talented at the sewing machine, dresses for girls, little and big, will look and wear better than the department-store variety. Few teen girls wear dresses to school, though, so the sewing may need to be limited to Sunday wear. "Will he/she wear this if I make it?" is a valid and often necessary question Grandma should ask the child's mother before buying the cloth and pattern.

And more than one grandma has eventually found herself drafted to make the bridesmaids' dresses for Granddaughter's wedding!

Consider the age and maturity of your grandchild when buying a gift. If you're tempted to purchase a genuine Swiss army knife (about $35) or a staghorn-handle hunting knife ($100 up) for a grandson, wait until he's a teen. The usual thing for pre-teen boys to do with pocket knives is to lose them within a month or so. He'll appreciate a Barlow knife ($1.98), however.

My two oldest sons were teens when they shared the cost of a .22-caliber single-shot rifle at a yard sale held by a grandfather several years ago. Sheepishly, this granddad told me how he'd bought the rifle new for his eight-year-old grandson months earlier—without first asking his daughter, the boy's mother, for permission. Understandably, the mother didn't think her child was old enough for such an adult toy!

I have my own criteria for buying gift firearms for kids, beyond clearing it with the parents. Target rifles (.22's, ordinarily) should never be repeaters. This considerably reduces the chance of kids making mistakes with loaded guns. BB guns (air rifles) are no-no's because children may treat them like toys, though they often put out eyes and they can be fatal. No handguns for kids, ever.

I started my own boys on a shotgun. The range is far less than a .22, and the kick and roar of a shotgun will remind a kid that they're handling a deadly weapon each time they touch the shooting iron off! Of course many grandparents oppose kids owning guns, period, and that's all right, too. But some grandparents *will* buy guns for rural youngsters or those with access to a target range, so it only seems sensible to establish some guidelines.

It's a common mistake, whether your gift will be books, toys, clothing, or whatever, to wait until the flyers advertising Christmas specials arrive with the Sunday newspaper, then rush off to buy what's on sale. Such buying may address the "thought" in the heart of the giver; but since little thought may have been given to the need of the grandchild who will be the recipient, the gift may be discarded—or returned and exchanged.

◆

*But, it's the thought
that counts, isn't it?*

I can hear readers musing on *that* notion, almost in an audible murmur. Yes, indeed! Christ said of Mary of Bethany, who "wasted" the valuable alabaster box of ointment of spikenard on his feet, "Let her alone: against the day of my burying hath she kept this" (see Matt. 26:6-13; Mark 14:3-9; John 12:3-7). Jesus was not glorying in Mary's apparent groveling, like some earthly potentate who insists on sitting on a chair above his cowering subjects. Rather, looking into her heart, he could see her contrite, thoughtful, worshipful attitude which needed to express itself in this beautiful act of obeisance.

Yet the act of giving, if thought out intelligently, aims first of all to meet the need of the grandchild, the receiver. And in that giving, we should aim to please. Realistically, there was nothing Mary could have given Jesus shortly before his crucifixion that he needed more than this act of worship in preparation for his burial.

"She hath done what she could," Jesus acknowledged (Mark 14:8).

"I don't care what they want; I'm good at fruitcakes, so I'm making fruitcake" is hardly a *thought* of love, though the act itself may be appreciated, certainly. Be sure your heart, head, your purse, and the needs of your grandchildren all coincide. You'll be a glad grandparent bearing gifts at Christmastime—or at any other time!

14

Parenting Is for Parents

"**M**other, I've tried that. Amy's rash just *won't* clear up!" Sandy's indignation at her mother's offer of a tube of hydrocortisone cream for six-month-old Amy's rash, which had spread even to body areas always kept dry and exposed to fresh air, was largely frustration at the ineffectiveness of salves and creams to stop this scarlet plague.

"When did it begin?" ventured Amy's grandma, casting a worried look toward the baby, who looked badly sunburned, though she had not been in the sun.

"Just over a week ago, when I took her off the breast. And I'm following the pediatrician's formula *exactly*," Sandy insisted, anticipating her mother's next question.

"Then you don't think it's in Amy's system?"

"How *could* it be? I mix her formula with bottled spring water, and her baby food has *no* chemical additives. That's why I quit nursing in the first place. I found out the meat John and I were eating was raised on steroids, and I was afraid my milk would hurt the baby."

Grandma, who herself had become a vegetarian for a while during a brief fling with the flower children in the sixties, listened to Sandy elaborate on her favorite topic.

"Mrs. Theonas, that little old Yugoslavian lady that's moved in next door suggested I try *goat's* milk—can you imagine?"

"You can buy it at that Greek deli downtown," Grandma answered, half amused, half in earnest.

"Mother!"

"Really, now, you had a rash, too. We switched from cows' milk to soybean formula until you were two. It cleared right up."

"I *won't* mess with what I put in Amy's system until she sees the doctor!"

Grandma changed the subject.

A week later, Sandy phoned, ecstatic. "Guess what, Mom? Doctor Walcott put Amy on soybean formula. Her rash cleared right up—even the diaper rash is gone!"

"No goat's milk?"

"*That's* a funny question. The doctor said that should work, too, if I could find it in the stores."

◆

Fifty dollars to learn from a doctor what two grandmas already knew,

Grandma thought as she hung the phone up. "I guess those kids have to learn these things for themselves," she sighed aloud to nobody but herself.

176

Grandmas, from little, old Yugoslavian ladies to sophisticated suburban dames wise in all the knowledge of American childrearing from Dr. Spock to Dr. Dobson, are vast reservoirs of knowledge, oozing with advice many young mothers ignore. Grandpas also seem to know more than fathers could ever hope to learn. We made *our* mistakes. Why should our grandchildren suffer when all this accumulated wisdom is on tap?!

Shirley Franks, mother of ten and grandmother of twenty-two, advises that "Mostly you think about what you'd like to say or what you'd like to do" when your children are making decisions affecting your grandchildren. Grandma Shirley, in fact, only "hinted about the inadvisability" of letting her newly licensed, sixteen-year-old grandchild have a car to commute to school, though a bus was available. Then "I bit my tongue," she chuckles. Within a few days the parents learned by expensive trial and error that Grandma was right.

Grandma, glad that she had not indulged in a lecture beforehand, followed by an "I told you so" afterward was prayerfully happy that her grandchild was unhurt.

But married children "Don't forget how you've brought *them* up," notes Shirley. As the years pass, your children go through the same things with their children that you went through with them. Grandparents who have maintained a happy rapport with their adult children will from time to time find that they "check you out to see if you'd still make the same decisions," she says. This permits grandparents to tactfully have a direct input into family decisions without being offensive.

"No grandparent has the right to take away from fathers and mothers the right to do their own parenting," author Charlie W. Shedd, himself a grandfather, comments *(Grandparents: Then God Created Grandparents, and it was Very Good,* Doubleday, 1976.) Shedd's salient wisdom is based on this truth: Experience *is* the most effective teacher, though it's often not the kindest! Our children, now parents themselves, have already been "train(ed) *up*" by us. As Shirley Franks observes, they continue to mature as they apply what we've taught them while young to living situations, modifying our teachings to suit the needs of a new generation. And while there are many timeless, practical truths not requiring specialized medical expertise—grandmas know that some infants whose systems cannot tolerate cows' milk will thrive on goats' milk or soy formula, for example—life does constantly change. Adult children do often speak the truth when they insist that "It's not the same world we grew up in."

So, how does a grandparent—who really *does* know things about child-rearing perhaps not even guessed by a young parent—go about imparting this wisdom to married adult children with kids (other than by writing a book!)? Here are some hints:

◆

*Don't offer advice on sensitive
topics unless invited to do so.*

Notice that by suggesting, "Then you don't think it's in Amy's system?" Sandy's mother tactfully drew out Sandy's opinion, while expressing just enough of her own to let her daughter know that there was more in her mind if Sandy wished to enquire.

◆

Realize that your son-in-law or daughter-in-law was probably reared by parents who had quite different sets of unspoken signals than you are familiar with,

even though they may be studiously polite in your presence. For instance, a young parent reared by parents from the South may have learned that it's impolite to disagree under any circumstances. But in the Northeast friendly disagreements are a means of intellectual stimulation! Does your in-law's silence mean he/she is anticipating a friendly debate—or is he/she trying to avoid what they may perceive to be an unpleasant argument brewing? A person unused to debate can easily lapse into lost temper when faced with disagreement; whereas a person whose conversation style is debative may be perceived as rude when he continues on to the next point. Learn these differences before you put your ideas, however pertinent, out for airing!

◆

*Learn to separate sensitive,
personal advice from impersonal advice.*

And realize that what you may consider impersonal may be taken personally by a person of differing thought processes. To point out that your son-in-law's car, which is belching black smoke, probably needs the choke cleaned may be taken as suggesting he's a polluter and somewhat of a slob; that your son-in-law, ordinarily meticulous about auto maintenance, is becoming lax; or he may be grateful to know that a stuck choke can sometimes be fixed with a $1.59 can of solvent and an old toothbrush since a mechanic has just quoted $300 for a carburetor overhaul which his car may not need.

One mother might gladly welcome advice about how to cure a baby's rash, yet she may find advice on educating that same child offensive and overwhelming. Another mother might be offended at either level of advice; a third, at neither.

◆

*Is your grandchild going to be seriously
harmed by your withholding advice?*

Not usually. "You really should see an orthodontist about Tommy's crooked teeth," you remark. But Tommy's mother, who has discussed this with the family dentist already, has valid reasons for *not* spending the

$3,000 on orthodontics—she wants to put it away for his education. She knows Tommy has lots of friends, so his teeth are no hindrance to him socially. And she has a close friend, who, after great expense on her son's teeth, saw him lose several in a ballgame.

◆

*Do you have constructive solutions
to what you perceive to be a problem?*

Or are you just airing complaints or worries? "I'm afraid for little Ritchie with all those trucks rumbling past your house," you may say. But what do you propose? Should Mother keep Ritchie indoors at all times? Tether him to a tree? Spank him soundly for playing near the road? Teach him to fear trucks (cars, though quieter, are just as dangerous!)?

Instead, "Could you folks use a fenced back yard? Your father's been wanting an excuse to use that new band saw in the garage. He'll saw the pickets any style you like, and I think we've got enough money in our rainy day account to buy the lumber," could be a happy and appropriate solution to Mother's dilemma with little Ritchie and traffic danger.

◆

*Before you speak, recall advice from
a grandparent that you wish you'd heeded
when raising your own children.*

My mother, my grandchildren's great-grandmother, can't remember when she could not read. Her own mother, a teacher before 1920 when most youngsters were taught reading by the phonetic method, introduced her to letters and sounds. Her earliest memories include reading news reports in the *Daily Kennebec Journal* (Augusta, Maine). Mother began school in grade four at age nine.

So when our daughter was not quite four, we were introduced to a Christian school pre-K reading program which had four-year-olds reading fifth and sixth grade books easily and with comprehension by the phonetic method. Our Debbie was three years, ten months old when she began school—which her grandmother did not think was a good idea! By her fourth birthday, she could read the King James Bible—and so could most of her classmates.

Would I recommend the same thing for my grandchildren? Not on your life! Studies by Dr. Raymond Moore, the nation's leading Christian home-school advocate, indicate that children should not be inducted into classroom schooling until they are at least seven; ten is better. So my grandchildren's great-grandmother, at nine, began school at an ideal age. My grandchildren's great-great-grandmother, a young mother whose education consisted of a year of college (normal school) and whose only experience was as a Maine school marm in a one-room school, made the right choice without the learned advice of Dr. Moore.

Two generations later I made the wrong choice, and Debbie, myself, and her mother—now Grandma Wiggin—have learned a great deal which we'd have missed had we not had the chance to choose, even when choosing badly. Would I have listened to my mother had she more strenuously advised me not to start my children in school so young? Of course not! I was proud of my college education, but she was *only* a high school graduate. Furthermore, evangelical Christian schools were a new movement, unheard of in most of America when Mother had school-age youngsters. What, I thought, could she possibly know?!

So, if my daughter and daughter-in-law wish to keep their youngsters home until they're emotionally ready, more power to 'em. Grandpa Wiggin may even lend them a phonetic reader and gently, very gently suggest that four-year-olds can be *home*-taught to read, as was their great-grandmother.

◆

*You might be considered
to be meddling,*

even when a family seems completely out of control and badly appears to need your wisdom. Your good advice could even make things worse in the long run. Let's say a divorce is imminent. You say, "Throw the bum out! Don't let him treat you and the kids like that!" By doing this, you may have touched the apple of your daughter's eye—her love for her estranged husband, however fractured it is—right while she's struggling with a heartrending decision.

Rather, give her love and support, if you want her in your life when it's over. And remember, your son-in-law is not beyond redemption. He may yet get his life straightened out and become an effective father to your grandchildren, even after the divorce.

◆

Give your married children room to grow into their child-rearing responsibilities.

One day when I, my parents' eldest, was about sixteen, in an indignant moment of self-pity I asked my father why he allowed one of my younger siblings to get away with thus-and-so without getting his impudent hide tanned. "I've learned a few things since you were small," he answered archly. Does it surprise you that one of my own older children has asked the same question about why tag-along Brad, who arrived after a seven-year hiatus in our childbearing, gets away with anything short of homicide?

◆

*Remember that God
is still in control*

of your children and grandchildren who are yielded to his will. But you can and should pray!

The Lord puts opposites together to balance a marriage, including the child-rearing process. If both your grandchildren's parents are following the Lord, can you trust him to use this natural tension (opposites attract) to bring about stability and balanced child-rearing?

15

Are Today's Kids Different?

I'm an old fogey. Brad, fifteen, won't say that, exactly, but he suspects it's true—part of the time he thinks so, at least.

Brad is our tagalong, after-40 child. Dot and I, grandparents four times, are old enough to be *his* grandparents. We're also old enough to notice some dramatic differences between Brad and his friends and the teen friends of his oldest brother and sister, a half-generation ago. Since returning to the classroom as a substitute teacher and after living in an adult world for many years, I've noticed some subtle changes.

◆

Today's teens fit a unique mold—with both same and different problems as teens of other eras.

They are more candid about sex than kids were when your children were growing up. This can range from the brash, coarse, and vulgar to merely discussing homosexuality candidly as an abstraction (forbidden and shocking when I was a teen). It takes a wise grandparent, sometimes, to know when a child is opening up on the topic of sex because he honestly wants an adult opinion, or because he's defying convention with the shock value of his words.

Today's teens, on the whole, are less rebellious toward cultural mores and parental values than teens of the sixties and seventies but more rebellious than those of the forties and fifties. This may surprise a grandparent, particularly one who fell asleep in 1957 and awoke in 1993 to find himself the grandpa or grandma of a teen guy or girl. Recently I mentioned to one of my young adult children that *Seventeen,* a Christian film shot in the 1950s, featured a daredevil game of "chicken" played with hot rods on a back road. One of the film's teens was killed.

"Dad, get real," he said when I inquired if kids still do crazy stuff like that today. "That was for bombed-out druggies of your generation. Nobody today'd be that stupid!" Of course he was equating me with the hippie movement mentality fostered by the first wave of baby boomers (born 1946-1964); I predate that by a few years!

Teens of the 1960s and 1970s were exposed to Timothy Leary and LSD, Woodstock and nude drug parties. They had unisex hairdos and clothes, and the Beatles. They were also idealists, seeking answers to social problems, such as the cause of war, to a degree not found among either my generation or among today's youth.

But though miniskirts are popular again, many girls do wear modest dresses to school, and they're not ridiculed for it, either. Rather than bare legs with short skirts, many teen girls today save their miniskirts for freezing temperatures—then wear them over a pair of men's long-handled drawers! Teens of the 1990s, lacking the explosive, change-the-world philosophy of the "Now Generation" of thirty years ago, are more apt to conform than rebel, though they tend to conform more to teen culture and less to the values of their parents than did the generation of their grandparents in the 1940s and 1950s. What girl years ago would wear men's underwear as an outer garment, for example?!

Many of today's teen girls have been caught in the fringes of feminism and women's rights, but few have been drawn into its core. Girls today are much more likely to smoke (guys less), slightly more likely to have experienced sex (but not as likely as the sexperts claim who trot out statistics which include married eighteen- and nineteen-year-olds to support public school sex ed), and more likely to repeat a risque story than girls of a few years ago. And while decency groups have been publicly combating pictorial porn aimed at men and boys, printed pornography has quietly slipped into the novels found in public libraries and some school libraries. Many teen girls are heavy readers of this type of illicit diversion.

But today's girls still say "thank you" if you hold the door for them, wear skirts to church and other dress-up occasions, and they are still given to feminine hairdos and romantic fantasies about proms, silk gowns, low lights and loud music. And let someone's big sis bring her baby to class, and most girls will crowd around to hold it as shamelessly as groupies after a rock singer!

Brad and I were coming out of a convenience store one Saturday evening as an auto full of teen girls pulled away. "That's odd," I remember observing.

"What's that?"

"Four girls—no guys."

"So?"

"When I was your age, that was a rare sight."

"Didn't girls drive cars then?"

"Sure—your mother had one."

Writing in *The Closing of the American Mind,* the epochal study of American attitudes in the late twentieth century, Allen Bloom notes that dating is going out of fashion in many circles. Many of today's youth, having had their self-confidence damaged through the divorces of their parents, fear being alone with an individual of the other sex. So they choose the security of the herd, instead. You see groups of girls, groups of guys, mixed groups, but a lot less pairing than years ago.

Possibly a teen feels as naked on his first date as on the wedding night. I doubt that that's an overstatement, for all the old, hidden fears of who one is and what one is in the eyes of a significant other come to the surface with a rush of blush when one is alone for the first time with that guy or girl. And many of today's teens simply will not single date, which may partly explain later marriages.

The child of divorce, not having two parents who love each other to build his or her confidence toward the other sex, often lacks the courage to face the trauma of being alone with a member of the other sex. With roughly half of all marriages ending in divorce (the divorce rate peaked in 1981), the impact on teen society is such that today's teens, even those from solid homes, must deal with the consequences of the emotional and social insecurity this phenomenon has brought about. Your teen grandchild, though he may not have had parents who were divorced, is nonetheless a part of this culture, and he shares much of the herd mentality common today.

Brad was surprised, for instance, to learn that, time was, it was unusual to see large numbers of teens in groups on a weekend evening. When I was his age, guys or girls would run in groups in the afternoon; by evening, most paired off. Parties, in those days were centered around couples—even though our parents often resisted this practice, fearing promiscuity.

The teen from a divorced home, notes "Focus on the Family" (April 19, 1992), suffers a "diminished ability to form lasting relationships."

He is more likely to divorce later; or before marriage, to drift into cohabitation, which sets him up for a 50 percent higher than average divorce rate, according to sociologists at the University of Wisconsin and Johns Hopkins University.

Teen guys, as well as girls, are more candid about sex than a few years ago. But there is more gallantry and less boorishness toward girls than twenty or thirty years ago. Compared to the forties and fifties, however, when many boys were patterning their manners after the likes of Clark Gable and Humphrey Bogart, boys today are less outwardly romantic. Among some, though, there's a nasty undercurrent of sexual pursuit which on the surface seems to come straight from the *Playboy* philosophy. But if you look behind the scenes, it's apparent that a lot of today's attitudes are a reaction to role-switching between Mom and Dad at home, which in turn may be a product of young mothers denying their maternal instincts in favor of outside employment.

Short haircuts on guys are back, and today's teen girls are more interested in a guy with a hairy chest and bulging biceps than, as in the 1960's, attracted to the fellow with the flowing mane, beads, and platform shoes. This may seem odd to grandparents whose exposure to youth culture has been a furtive glance at MTV while changing channels. Tentatively, I'll suggest that the reason so many male rock stars still effect the effeminity common twenty years ago is that their philosophy is borrowed directly from the LSD-dropping hippies of the 1960s.

Yet there's a dark side to this, also. Many of today's girls, in searching for images of manhood lost in absent fathers, have found it in raw sensuality. The likes of the male strippers featured on the morning talk shows are found in the tanned, all-but-naked male "hunks" taped inside girls' lockers lining the corridors of public high schools.

Guys' clothing is back to the masculine, with elements borrowed from their grandparents and parents in a medley unique to the 1990s. Time was, a guy who wore sneakers to school was called square. Double so, if he wore dungarees and a polo shirt. When you and I were young, *de rigueur* for guys was a plaid shirt, sharply creased cotton twill trousers, a narrow belt, penny loafers, and white athletic socks; a crew cut (flat top!), close on the sides, or a Princeton, for guys blessed with manageable hair; a narrow tie, if you dressed up. Girls wore white socks, too, with loafers or saddle shoes. But sneakers and jeans were strictly athletic gear, except for farm kids.

Todays' teens consider loafers "preppie"; kids in upper-middle-class schools wear them, but in working-class neighborhoods they are scorned. For a pair of jeans the average teen will spend what could buy Grandpa a fine pair of wool dress trousers—even if he has to pawn his rollerblades and wrist watch to do so. Today's teen clothing is unisex only insofar as both guys and girls prefer jeans, except for dress-up occasions. Girls ordinarily wear their jeans or skirts with feminine blouses or tee shirts. Guys wear polo shirts or tee shirts. A lot of girls are seen with pedal-pusher length jeans, fancy embroidery at the legs. Sneakers, usually jogging or tennis variety, are universal, except in upper-middle-class schools, where loafers are worn in mild weather and Bean boots in the snow season.

◆

*Today's youth of both sexes are more
peer dependent than ever before.*

And they have more money to spend than ever—or
their parents do. Guys and girls both will spring
hundreds on prom clothes, even to a chauffeured limo
and a fancier party than a wedding, if possible. For many
youth today, the prom has become *the* rite of passage
into adulthood. For some, it ends with sex in a motel
room. A lot of parents give tacit assent to such all-night
parties, closing their minds to what obviously goes on in
a rented motel room. And with Christian parents, the
prom is of itself a problem to be dealt with, since it
involves dancing, rock music, and ungodly associations.

Few of today's teens are addicted to drugs, and drug
usage among the young is actually down from a few
years ago. Most have tried marijuana, though, and one or
more types of pills. Alcohol, usually beer, but sometimes
wine coolers, is still the drug of choice for teens. And in
this matter, it's like father, like son, ordinarily. A study of
New York City high schoolers reported in *Time* showed
drug use among teens to be directly proportional to alcohol and tobacco use with their parents. In homes
where neither of the parents smoked, drank, or used
drugs, the use of drugs or alcohol was seldom a problem
with teens in the home either.

Young people nowadays have access to more
knowledge than any prior generation. For instance, more
scientific data has been accumulated during my lifetime

than was discovered and compiled during the thousands of years before my birth since the creation. Yet, paradoxically, the typical seventeen-year-old knows less about the world around him than did his recent ancestors, according to *What Do Our 17-Year-Olds Know: A Report on the First National Assessment of History and Literature* by Diane Ravitch and Chester E. Finn, Jr. Today's high schooler is exposed to tons of propaganda which passes for education; much of the curricula in many classrooms is thin on facts and larded with political opinion—written and taught, not surprisingly, by the Now Generation activists of the 1960s!

Today's teens of both sexes have healthier bodies, eat better, breathe cleaner air, and dress better than their parents or grandparents. Youth in the 1990s are concerned about ecology, AIDS, and abortion; their parents, by contrast were largely concerned about war (Vietnam) and civil rights. Their grandparents' concern, I'm ashamed to admit, was largely in making money.

Many of us recall Billy Graham preaching against materialism in the 1950s—our generation! Graham was right, then. But materialism is popular again, and youth with all its idealism has not escaped it.

"Mike just got a new mountain bike," Brad said the other day. My ears perked up. "Paid $600 for it, too!"

I knew that Mike's family, who attend our church, is a large one. Though Mike's dad is steadily employed, his car is as rusty as mine, so I asked, "Where'd he get that kind of money?"

"Mike's got a job," Brad indignantly answered.

"I had a job when I was fifteen, too," I prodded, remembering that I barely made enough to keep tires on my beat-up Columbia bike and buy school clothes, with a little left over for treats.

"He sold his snowboard. Got $200 for it."

"For a snowboard?"

"Yeah. He paid over $300 for it two years ago."

"You paid $200 for your mountain bike two years ago," I reminded Brad. I reminded him also that he'd told me recently that his bike was now priced $600 new, and that a year ago he spent $100 from his paper route having it upgraded with the latest accessories.

"But I couldn't get more'n $100 if I were to sell it."

"That's not the point. What's it worth to you?"

"It *is* a better bike than Mike's," Brad admitted at last, still using a materialistic measure of his wheels' worth.

It's comparatively easy to teach a child like Brad the value of money in economic terms. He knows, for instance, that his $200 used, high-quality bike is a better deal than one that sells for $99.95 new, which will self-destruct within a year.

But to teach a teen eternal values in regard to money, sex, and a myriad assortment of other issues is the real challenge. What Brad and your grandchildren are seeking answers to, though many of them can't put words to their feelings, are not the lost causes of the 1940s and 1950s when we struggled to build an economic kingdom to avoid a repeat of the Depression of the 1930s; nor of the 1960s and 1970s, when youth—today's parents and teachers—sought to "make love, not war"; nor of the

1980s and 1990s, when spotted owls in Oregon timber forests and animals in Amazon rain forests have captured the imagination of youth.

Rather, more than at any time in life, teens—from Cain and Abel millenia ago, to Charlie and Andy who perhaps are tossing lay-ups in your backyard basketball court right now—seek to have their lives make sense, to find meaning and purpose. In this, teens never change; nor does the answer—submission to the claims of Christ on their lives.

Grandparents are encouraged when teens like Jonathan Wyrtzen, Jack Wyrtzen's grandson, accept the challenge to be different in the face of an often-hostile public school environment. As valedictorian of his 1992 senior class at Midlothian High School, near Dallas, Texas, Jonathan had a solid Christian testimony going back to his grade-school years.

On graduation day, Jonathan stood to give his speech to a crowd of some 2,000 parents, students, and friends—and his grandparents, Jack and Joan Wyrtzen. After warming his audience with several teen-style jokes, Jonathan turned serious. "Everybody is looking for one thing in life to make them happy. I have found that one thing," he said. "That one thing is Jesus Christ as my Lord and Savior."

The crowd of mostly nonbelievers gave Jonathan a standing ovation!

Two Bible teens, a girl who went wrong though she had her parents' affection, and the girl's teen half-brother who did right although hundreds of miles from home, illustrate the need for grandparents in the lives of teens—teens who are outwardly changed much from yesteryear, but who inwardly have needs and concerns which are ageless.

Fourteen-year-old Dinah, confused at her father's cowardice when confronted by his brother, disturbed by the bickering amongst her father and the two women in his life, strayed into premarital sex so vile in her brothers' eyes that they murdered her boyfriend and his family (see Gen. 34:1-2; 25-27).

Dinah's half-brother was Joseph, about her age at the time of this episode. Too young to have joined the older boys in their bloody raid to retrieve their sister, you can be sure he pondered this occurrence and its side effects for years afterward. And scorned by Dinah's brothers, Joseph was sold by them to a caravan of traders bound for Egypt.

About five years later, Joseph, now nineteen, rugged and handsome and overseer of wealthy Potiphar's household servants, was tempted by his employer's seductive wife. Though it could have cost him his life, Joseph slipped her forced embrace and ran out without his shirt. Evidently shamed by his wife's open lewdness, Potiphar preserved Joseph alive, but had him jailed to save face.

But for Joseph, sexual immorality was a sin, not only against Potiphar, who trusted and respected him, but against God who created sex and set bounds on its use (see Gen. 39:7-20).

Yet God remembered Joseph, so that eventually he became wealthy, successful, and able to repay his wicked half-brothers good for the evil they had done him (see Gen. 45:1-8)!

◆

Grandparents are given by God to fill in the gaps missed by the grandchildren's parents.

Some of us may have seen a daughter or granddaughter go the way of Dinah, flirting with guys not worthy of her, fooling with sex to fill the emptiness within her soul. Then we have our Josephs or Janies, teen grandchildren who, perhaps because of being misunderstood by their own generation and parents, as Joseph was, or for longings which they can put no words to, open up to us. Our opportunity is to hear what their parents did not hear, to see what their busy parents missed. Perhaps it is only a pat on the back they need or a word of encouragement from the Bible. Perhaps, like Potiphar, we've seen in that grandchild a youth who wants our direction on a long-term basis, and we hire them to weed our garden, to wax our car; or we take them hunting or fishing or become their tutor in homework through a difficult year in high school. Perhaps, like Pharaoh, we can be used of the Lord to give a grandchild a boost on the climb to successful living before God.

Other grandparents, like Jack and Joan Wyrtzen, need only to write letters, to phone, to pray, and to be on hand for graduations and other special occasions because Mom and Dad have built into that child/grandchild's life the courage to be positively different!

16

When Love Must Say "No"

My son Mark, then fifteen, waited outside his Grandma Wiggin's front door, a perturbed but polite police officer behind him in the shadows. "This your grandson?"

"He sure is!" Grandma was concerned, though looking Mark over she could spy no signs of injury.

"We got a call from one of your neighbors that a prowler was shining a flashlight onto their house." The policeman produced a two-cell light.

"That's my flashlight. I loaned it to him," Grandma affirmed quickly. "What were you doing?" she addressed Mark.

"Minding his own business, near's I could tell," the officer answered for him. "But lots of people get suspicious if they see someone outside with a light. Figure they might be setting them up for a burglary."

"But Mark's only . . . "

"I know. He's from out of town, and he's hardly a burglary suspect. But it might be best to leave the flashlight in the house from now on. Thank you, ma'am." The cop handed my mother the flashlight and strode off to his patrol car.

Having a grandson brought to your door by a uniformed officer is an unnerving experience, and fortunately it rarely happens to most of us.

Mark is the father to two of my grandchildren now, and this vignette from his past is a family joke. He had grown up beyond the street lights, and when he went out at night he often carried a flashlight. Visiting Grandma in a strange city neighborhood, he asked to borrow her flashlight, and she lovingly said "Yes" without hesitation. He'd innocently cast a light beam on a stray cat scurrying after a mole. So now she'd have to say "No."

Not a few grandparents lock horns with teen grandchildren visiting in their homes. This can easily occur when the teens have grown up miles from the grandparents, and neither teen nor grandparent knows what to expect of the other. Misunderstandings may range from problems with innocent but inappropriate behavior to actions that startle or shock the sensibilities of a grandparent or even to conduct that flouts morality.

Generally kids act much better for teachers and grandparents than at home. There's something about a new relationship that causes even the child who's a dickens at home to behave better for a person with whom he's not yet plumbed the depths of their authority. I think it's a combination of family respect, subconscious wishes to protect the parents' good name, and respectful fear of unknown authority that makes this so.

For a child under age eleven or twelve, your control must be *in loco parentis*—in the parent's place. Behavior standards should be worked out beforehand, either tacitly or explicitly, with your grandchild's parents. Grandma may wish to adjust rules to suit circumstances, of course. For instance, a nine o'clock bedtime for a nine-year-old may be enforced at home because Mom and Dad, who rise at six, wish to be alone for an hour before bedtime. But Grandma, who sleeps until eight, may let little Willie stay up until ten thirty to beat her at chess, if there's no school tomorrow.

Puberty, however, brings on a new set of standards for dealing with children. A pre-teen or teenager is struggling with a combination of childhood dependency and emerging adult independence. One day Susie, at ten, is a child, playing mother with dolls. At eleven or twelve, she's probably become physically capable of *being* a mother, preening herself for boyish glances (she sees boys under fifteen as hopelessly immature), and she's put her dolls on the shelf. But she still sleeps with her Teddy bear! By age fifteen or sixteen youth of both sexes think adult thoughts, and they sense that they have been caught between adulthood and childhood. They are vulnerable to impulsive, sometimes surly behavior to demonstrate their independence. Unless given an uncommon amount of parental support, they may vent this frustration in inappropriate ways.

When teens or college-age grandchildren are your houseguests, therefore, it's up to you to help them set boundaries. In some instances you'll need to consult their parents, of course. Here are some situations which may require you to say "No."

◆

Church attendance should be required
of teens visiting grandparents.

This should be understood in advance so the teen will bring clothing appropriate to the occasion. It's probably unfair for you to expect your teen grandchild to attend church if their carry-along wardrobe consists of a pair of jeans with the knees out and a bathing suit. But if they're used to wearing jeans to church, in good humor let them wear them. "It's no skin off your nose to wear a tie," I once told Mark when he protested a regulation at his Christian high school which neither of us agreed with. Conversely, it's no skin off Grandma's nose if Eddie—or Susie—wants to go to church in jeans. Isn't the important thing that they be exposed to the spiritual environment and the teaching of the Word of God?

◆

Make allowances for denominational differences
and established church-attendance habits.

Courtesy is a two-way street. If you are a Baptist or Assemblies of God and your son or daughter has married an Episcopalian (or vice-versa) and is rearing your grandchildren in this denomination, compassionately realize that your grandchildren may be uncomfortable in a worship service with practices that are strange to them. Don't insist they accompany you to every service, though you should insist they keep the biblical principle of worship in the house of God at least once weekly. Try this: Offer them a choice among Sunday school, morning worship, or evening service. They may surprise you and choose all three!

◆

Don't push clothing requirements

beyond what's necessary for decency, ordinarily. Your teen's parents might be more stringent with dress requirements than this of course, but kids should be able to relax at Grandfather's Mountain. I require young men to remove their caps or hats and wear shirts at mealtime. But that's a table rule, not a clothing rule, *per se*. (I don't let them sit on the table, either!)

If you find fifteen-year-old Susie's bikini or high-cut one-piece suit too brief for public beach wear (another issue which should be discussed with her mother beforehand), insist she wear something more modest. In a pinch, she might wear shorts or cut-off jeans with the suit, for example. Susie is probably not unreasonable to want to wear a skimpy suit in the back-yard pool if there are no men around and she agrees to dress or wear a robe when she is done with her swim, however.

Grandmothers who grew up when girls covered up simply because they were told to do so may not realize that young people today expect more explanation for rules than in the past. And even with the exposure to sex teens get in school, girls' magazines, and in the movies, many girls do not actually realize what they are doing to males—sixteen or sixty-six—by such casual exposure until they've been taught. It's entirely appropriate for Grandma to speak to Susie in private and point out what Christ said about looking to lust (see Matt. 5:28) or the result of Bathsheba's careless bathing and King David's longing looks (see 2 Sam. 11:2-5).

◆

Smoking, drinking and drugs are not permitted in Grandma's house.

It should make little difference whether it's Eddie, seventeen, or his father, forty-seven, on this one. But precedent sometimes must be honored to keep family peace. If there are smokers in your family and you've permitted them to smoke indoors over the years, it may be too late to change the rules without hurt and anger. About all you can do is inquire with the parents if they permit their teens to smoke at home, then make them smoke outside until they reach the legal age for smoking, eighteen. But if their parents have a "no smoking" rule at home, they should not even be permitted to smoke out-doors. And if you've never permitted smoking in the house, there's no reason to let it start—ever. So if twenty-year-old Junior comes home from college with a pipe in his mouth, insist he take it outdoors, even if it's twenty below zero.

But no booze—beer, wine coolers, or hard liquor—is permitted under any circumstances. And teens, or even over-twenty-one college-age youths who may drink legally, should not be permitted to go out and drink, say, at a bowling alley with a bar, while they are visiting Grandma and Grandpa.

◆

*Music and TV should
be controlled.*

Here's where younger teens, even from otherwise solid Christian homes will run over you if you let them, and in some respects it's an iffy situation for grandparents of teens. You will not permit morally objectionable music and TV programs, of course. But, say you've got cable TV because Grandpa likes historical documentaries, and the package comes with MTV and late-night R-rated movies. State up front that MTV, with its suggestive, often lewd, visuals and lyrics, is not to be turned on, and no movies after the eleven o'clock news. Post this rule conspicuously on every TV set in the house, and remind the teens that it will be enforced. And grandparents should set the example by not tuning in to the daytime soaps. And perhaps Grandpa could miss a few TV ballgames to build a relationship with Eddie by playing ball with him in the back yard!

Rock music is an addiction with many teens that grandparents frequently must deal with. Dr. James Dobson observes that "a steady diet" of hard rock "will pollute the minds of even the healthiest teenagers" (Focus on the Family, August 1992). While Dobson's observation has to do with lyrics which he found often violent and explicitly sexual, the music with or without the words will drive a lot of grandparents into near insanity. It should be part of your teen's maturing process to learn to respect the rights of others who do not wish to be subjected to his or her favorite sounds. Insist that he shut it off or at least wear headphones. Medical reports have shown that a radio or tape player cranked up to where it can be heard by those not wearing the headset is damaging the listener's ears. That's the bottom line on volume.

So, must Grandma scrutinize each and every tape Eddie or Susie play in their Walkmans? It's not feasible. But this may require parental contact, and in some instances, a truce. Try limiting the teen to gospel music only when at Grandma's house. If it's a modern piece that grates on your nerves, listen to some of it anyway, and let him explain what the words mean to him. Then relegate it to earphone-only listening.

◆

Teens must keep regular hours
at Grandma's house.

And they should be expected to phone if delayed by an emergency. "But Grandma, I'm almost an adult. *You* don't call when you're late!" is Susie's accusation at seventeen. She's just got her driver's license, and you let her go to the supermarket at eight in the evening for a box of cereal. She met a friend she hadn't seen all summer, and they went to McDonald's and stayed until after ten.

First, shame on Grandma! Jay Kesler, president of Taylor University and former president of Youth for Christ, says that his secretary can reach him on a half-hour notice even when he's traveling overseas. If *you* went to the store and got delayed two hours, you owe Susie (or Grandpa!) a call, too, out of ordinary courtesy. Then be back when you say you'll be back.

Try this. Point out to Susie that if you didn't love her you wouldn't be concerned. Make your own good practice an example. Teens often perceive curfews as unfair means to control them. "You wouldn't want someone telling you what to do," is an indignant, immature objection.

So appeal to their sense of responsibility. Insist they call home. And when they do, don't snap, "You come home this minute!" Ask, "When will you be home?" Then don't let them go out again for a while if they don't keep their word. This is an appeal to the maturity they profess to have rather than the exercise of your real, or imagined, urge to control.

Say "No" to letting a grandchild under age twenty-five drive your car

until you've cleared it with your insurance agent and (if under eighteen) with his or her parents. You can be held legally responsible for any damage he or she may do. In most cases your insurance will probably cover your grandchild to the same extent as you are covered without paying an extra premium, but state laws and insurance policies vary. If the grandchild is living in your home, however, you *must* pay extra for insurance. And you should not be bashful about asking him to pay it.

◆

Set bottom lines for moral behavior.

No grandparent should ever let his house or apartment become a crash pad where teen or college-age grandchildren can carry on premarital sex. This can be a problem, especially if your grandchild's parents are divorced or your grandson or granddaughter has had on-going troubles at home. Teens sometimes seek recourse from their problems by having sexual encounters, especially in these days of steady sexual fare on TV and in the movies. Your grandchildren should know, or you should tell them, that they are expected to refrain from sex, including petting and prolonged kissing, until marriage;

and they must understand that this is a rule which will be enforced while they're your guests.

Grandchildren should not be permitted to entertain guests of the opposite sex in their bedrooms, ever, no matter how old they are. Nor should they be permitted to sit in a car in the driveway for extended periods—and make this clear in advance. (Stock answers from teens confronted for spending two hours alone in a parked car: "Grandma/pa, we weren't *doing* anything—we were just talking"; or, "Nobody uses a car for *that* anymore!"

These answers may be truthful. Many times teen couples *will* sit and talk for long periods without getting physical. And many latchkey kids have turned to sex in the afternoon in bed at home, before the parents get home from work, or in motel rooms, instead of in parked cars. Kids quickly learn from school gossip what their friends are doing.

If your teen is visiting with a girl/boyfriend at your house, let them alone to watch the moon from the porch swing, if you have one. Or, give them reasonable privacy in the family room. Don't try to police every move, but be sure you're not a party to behavior they or their parents would later be ashamed of.

"Don't you trust me?" a teen grandchild may ask. "Yes, honey, I trust you. But I also love you more than you can imagine, so we've got to have rules," you may answer. Then let her or him help you formulate those rules.

◆

*Help your grandchildren say
"No" to sex before marriage.*

It may be that Susie or Eddie have sought out Grandma and Grandpa because their parents are so taken up with their own troubles that they have little emotional and spiritual strength left to share with their children. Love and compassion toward a teen grandchild developing into adulthood will often open the door to your helping that grandchild with their relationships with the opposite sex. Grandparents who obviously truly enjoy each other's company and who truly enjoy being around teen grandchildren are well on their way to helping teens realize that adults can relate to each other sexually in happy, wholesome relationships. If grandparents have an affectionate and caring relationship they can help teens understand that sex is okay and beautiful, but that it must wait for marriage.

Questions such as, "Grandma, when did you and Grandpa first kiss?" or "Tell me about your first date," can lead to gently pointing out that you were a virgin when you married Grandpa, and you've never regretted it.

Talk shows, such as Oprah Winfrey, produce panels of parents who state that it's all right with them if their kids have sex so long as it's at home while their parents are there to supply the condoms. Geraldo Rivera, who boasts of the well-known women he's bedded, recently interviewed a group of thirtysomething female rock singers who giggled about going to bed with male groupies as young as fourteen. And sweet-faced, squeaky clean show hostess Jenny Jones, with the help of authoritative, grandmotherly Dr. Joyce Brothers, encouraged a group of smirking, snickering middle-aged female entertainers in pajamas to tell her July '92 TV audience—many of them teen girls on summer vacation—about their exciting premarital sexual encounters (e.g. "on the football field with my boyfriend"). Is it any wonder that today's teens of both sexes face major confusion about morality?

Yet according to Dr. William R. Archer III, deputy assistant secretary for population affairs at the U.S. Department of Health and Human Services, 84 percent of ninth-grade girls (ages fourteen-sixteen) in an Atlanta program, Postponing Sexual Involvement, said that their "greatest need was learning how to say 'No' to their boyfriends." Kids of both sexes who go through the Atlanta program are "fifteen times less likely to be sexually involved," Archer found.

Woman's Day magazine surveyed thousands of sexually active women, married and single, teen through elderly. They found that women who attend church regularly, and who were virgins when they married, have sex more often and enjoy it more than non-religious women who lost their virginity before marriage.

And no wonder. When a couple unite in a sexual union—and you should tell your teens this—they become "one flesh," literally *one self* (see Gen. 2:24; Eph. 5:31). And this union or bonding is made whether or not the couple marry. When a man or woman give their virginity to the other, they have irretrievably given that person a piece of themselves (see 1 Cor. 6:15-16). Adam "knew" Eve and Eve "knew" Adam; they came to each other "naked . . . and not ashamed" of their nude bodies in a union of precious carnal knowledge not reproducible in any other human relationship (see Gen. 2:25; 4:1).

TV talk shows, newscasters, and many public schools, are promoting "safe sex" with a condom rather than teaching teens to say "No" until marriage basically because it's now taught as fact in most school science classrooms that your Eddie and Susie are animals, evolved from lower forms. If sex is only animal mating, then physical protection against AIDS or pregnancy is all that is necessary.

But the Christianity shared by you and your grandchildren gives sex a whole new dimension. As spiritual beings, humans intermingle souls ("know" each other) during sexual intercourse. And the only "safe sex" possible for spiritual beings is the lifetime covenant of marriage which the God who created and blessed sex intended! Even nature teaches that human sexuality is on a higher plane than the animals. Only human beings make love face to face!

Basic Youth Conflicts Seminars Director Bill Gothard suggests that girls, when asked for a date, respond, "I'll have to ask my daddy first." This puts dating and sex squarely in the context of family at the outset.

Sex is a secret to be shared by the two who are the basic unit of a family, not to be spread promiscuously about like water (see Prov. 5:15-21). Many a girl will enter a relationship with a guy for whom she "cares," chasing the fantasy that this "real" love is "forever." But if there's not been an "Until death do part us" commitment before the sex, that relationship soon dissolves, and she is left weeping with the pieces of her broken heart. Her next time around, whether in marriage or in another affair, she is wary, perhaps calloused. This, then, is the "No" message you should give your teen grand-daughters.

And what of grandsons? Possibly the most neglected passage in the New Testament is 1 Thessalonians 4:3-8, which ties holy living with sexual purity. Verse six stands as a somber warning against anyone who *takes advantage of* ("defrauds") another person sexually. When a guy takes a girl's virginity before they marry, he has cheated not only the girl, but her parents ("brother" in Christ) who entrusted her into his care. Such a young man has despised not only "man" (that is, the girl, her parents, and society) but God (see verse 8). This is the "No" your grandsons need to learn.

An excellent resource for grandparents dealing with teens about sex is *Why Wait: What You Need to Know about the Teen Sexuality Crisis* by Josh McDowell and Dick Day (Here's Life, 1987). This 444-page book is thorough and detailed. Teens should read it, too.

◆

Love may have to say "No"
to future visits

from your grandchild if basic codes of courtesy and conduct are not met. Such decisions are excruciating and should be made with prayer and reflective consideration. And make allowances for misunderstandings, of course.

But you have a responsibility before God to "restrain" teen or young adult grandchildren from morally objectionable behavior when they are in your home (1 Sam. 2:22; 3:13). You cannot condone wrongdoing by giving a grandchild a place in your home to carry it on. This kind of tough love can cause a youth to examine his or her behavior and shape up. Columnist Ann Landers reports, for example, instances where teens left off using drugs or running around at night when parents drew a line and refused to back down.

Grandparents can take a lesson from a popular slogan: quietly, calmly, firmly, lovingly "Just say 'No'" to behavior which violates the high standards you set for yourself and your family to the honor of the Lord.

17

Investing in Your Grandchildren's Future

Grandpa Hackney collected pennies in a piggy bank, and whenever my wife and I would visit her parents' home with our children, the bank would be dumped on the kitchen table and its contents counted. Those pennies bought ice cream cones, zoo tickets, rides on the plastic horsie at the supermarket. They furnished the seed money for a myriad assortment of gifts ranging from plush monkeys to rocking chairs.

The two of my four children who remember Grandpa Hackney are now parents themselves. Most of the gifts were long ago worn out and discarded, but the memory of this modestly indulgent grandfather is with them yet. Though Grandma Hackney, with more descendants than years, at eighty-four, tries her best to keep up with birthday gifts for grandchildren, great-grandchildren, and great-great-grandchildren—half of whom were born since Grandpa Hackney died—understandably, with nearly two family birthdays a week, she does miss one occasionally.

America's some fifty-five million grandparents spend about $550 apiece/$1,100 per couple per year on fewer than four grandchildren or on phone calls and travel to visit with grandchildren. And when today's grandparents pass on, since our nation's population has been aging at a time when the economy has been growing for most of the past half century, today's children and grandchildren will inherit more cash, investments, and real property than any generation in human history.

Our culture is a dichotomy where young families, many of whom have known only prosperous times, have overburdened themselves with consumer debt while grandparents—those who remember the Depression or who were influenced by parents who did—have set themselves up with tax-sheltered retirement plans in part in response to tax reforms in the past dozen years. Says Christian financial counselor Jim Rickard, director of Stewardship Services Foundation, "By the time parents become grandparents, with these corporate pension plans that have been in existence so long, retirees are becoming the strongest financial power bloc in the country."

My own grandparents, by contrast, though all of them owned property, passed little cash to their grandchildren while living, and they left none when they died. The real estate was passed to their children in return for care in old age. What possessions were left—a few pieces of furniture, books, bric-a-brac—were given to the grand-children in oral wills during the last days of their lives.

My grandparents made some mistakes in investing in their children's and grandchildren's futures, but for the most part, given their circumstances, time in life, and the economy at the time, I believe they made very good decisions.

My paternal grandparents were themselves from farm folks for several generations back, for instance, and they both grew to adulthood in the nineteenth century when a farmer could expect his sons and his sons' sons to follow in his footsteps. Grandpa Wiggin built a modest farm, which included a new, nicely furnished house—even indoor plumbing was installed some twenty years before the power lines ran out our way. He saw the passing of the horse and buggy, in middle age he bought a new car, and he helped both his sons with new or late-model wheels of their own. Old enough to be grandparents (my married aunt had no children) Grandpa and Grandma Wiggin had a baby boy in the same year they bought their first new car, a 1917 Willys-Overland tourer.

That baby was my father. At twenty-two, on the eve of World War II, my father was given the farm in ex-change for a life-lease in which he agreed to care for his parents to the end of their days. No cash was in-volved, nor did Grandpa Wiggin have any savings to speak of. And Grandpa stayed on the farm in his sunset years as adviser and helper.

Those halcyon days are gone forever. The twentieth century has seen more rapid economic and social changes than at any period in history, and the practice of father passing to son the farm or small business is no longer adequate to deal with inheritances. But from the good features of this time-honored practice we can glean lessons from grandparenting on into the twenty-first century.

"In the eyes of a grandchild, many times, a grandparent is put on a higher pedestal than even Mom and Dad," says Jim Rickard. This will occur only when grandparents, as mine were, are accessible on a regular basis. I'm sure I idolized my grandparents, especially Grandpa Wiggin. And as a young adult, I was often troubled by the fact that, as Rickard says, during the thirteen years that our lives overlapped I put him "on a higher pedestal than Dad." Grandpa was successful; Dad was still struggling to get there. Grandpa had a great past; Dad, to an extent, seemed to live in Grandpa's shadow. Only years after they both had passed on did I fully accept that both men did pretty much as well as could be expected in the context of opportunities in which God placed them.

Rickard paraphrases Proverbs 20:7, "If you want to raise children of integrity, be a model of integrity." Since grandparents *are* often looked up to as greater, in the eyes of grandchildren, than their parents, as grandparents we must accept this mantle of role-modeling. Grandparents must be men and women of their word in the presence of their grandchildren in regard to financial dealings. Whenever we handle money, there are impressionable eyes watching!

An example Rickard mentions is the frivolous use of credit cards before grandchildren, especially when it comes to buying them gifts. I don't recall ever knowing the *price* of anything my grandparents bought me, except a five-cent helium balloon at a fair, or a bottle of pop from my maternal grandfather's country store. Maybe that's not so good, either. Grandkids need to learn that neither cash nor gifts grow on trees!

Rickard gave the example of the indulgent grandparent who cruises the aisles of a department store with a child in tow, pushing a shopping cart. Gifts for the grandkid tumble into the cart. A plastic card is used to cover the bill at the cash register.

Suppose you *can* afford it? But can the grandchildren afford such a materialistic lesson? "The kids have no idea whatsoever that somebody's got to pay, that there's a day of reckoning," Rickard says. "They look to Grandma and Grandpa for freebies, for fun, instead of for reality."

Older youngsters do realize that credit-card purchases must be paid for, of course. But the easy-come-easy-go attitude of a grandparent sets an example of treating with frivolity the goodness of God from whom "every good gift and every perfect gift" originates (James 1:17).

Try this instead. Lay out in advance how much you plan to spend. Let the child see the money and perhaps count it. Pray with your grandchild, asking the Lord to lead you both to find your needs within the limits of available cash. Let him know that when it's gone, it's gone. If you can't trust yourself to stick with this decision, leave the rest of your cash, your checkbook, and your credit cards at home!

I recall that I had an appreciation for my grandparents' limited resources rather early in life. Grandpa Fuller, for instance, a part-time deputy sheriff, got paid five dollars for five or six hours' work keeping order at the local dance hall each Saturday night. I quite easily found myself relating his expenditures on his grandchildren to his modest stipend as a bouncer, a sum I could readily understand.

"I'm spending my grandchildren's inheritance," read the bumper sticker plastered on the rear of a motor home with Florida license plates. I'll admit I was not amused.

This is neither an indictment of owning a motor home nor wintering in Florida. Both practices raise some questions, though, which I have dealt with in another chapter. However, what does a grandparent's conspicuous consumption say to the grandchildren? To me it says, "You only live once. Get all the gusto you can. Tomorrow we die—there's no hereafter."

Grandparents who are alarmed at their grandchildren's indulgent living should not wrap themselves with the self-righteous cloak of, "He's spending it all when he's young; he won't have any left for old age" if they are themselves living as though old age were just a final vacation before annihilation. Can we live with eternity's values in view before our grandkids? In 1 Timothy 5:5-6 the Lord warns merry widows against living in pleasure because a life of indulgence is really death in life. What will such a life of pursuing the things of a dying world do to our grandchildren's attitudes toward money and possessions?

Another serious mistake is to give children or grandchildren large sums of money while they are young. A young son was left substantial endowments from his father's life insurance. This boy collected his endowments at age eighteen, about $75,000, which he spent within two years on new pickup trucks, motorcycles, and partying. Then, having no funds left for college, nor any particular training to land a decent job, he enlisted in the U.S. Navy.

Years later, this young man, now married and the father of two, is still in the Service. He plans to make a career of the military until he can retire on a pension. The military discipline, the guaranteed paycheck, the hope of a pension at age forty, are the things he now wants most in life. A regimented, structured life in which others tell him what to do and when to come and go is his future, for he has squandered his ability to discipline himself for any other kind of life. "What I could buy for my family if I had that money now," he was heard to complain.

Again, this is not a criticism of choosing a structured lifestyle, such as the military. But this young man was unable to manage money that might have paid for a college or trade-school education or have bought his family a house. Rickard tells of a Christian dad who's having second thoughts about the $500,000 he's stashed away at interest for his four-year-old to receive—perhaps $2 million by then—at age twenty-one.

There are many opportunities for grandparents with means to do so to help grandchildren with judiciously given gifts, even substantial ones.

◆

Invest in their
college education.

College tuition has increased much faster than the rate of inflation over the past thirty years. It's tough for families on the lower-middle-income level to put away money enough to pay their children's way, and in most cases nowadays it's impossible for a college student to pay his entire bill with a part-time job—community colleges excepted. The children of the poor do qualify for many free grants at state and federal levels, however.

Particularly if your children are in full-time Christian ministries, they may be unable to put away much toward a son or daughter's college expenses. It is entirely appropriate to help with their tuition bill, either on a regular basis, or with occasional lump-sum gifts as needed. Ordinarily, let your grandchildren know in advance how much to expect and when so he or she can plan accordingly.

◆

Some grandparents pay their grandkids'
way to a Christian day school.

This is an investment in your grandchild's future which can reap eternal dividends. Be sure that your grandchild really wishes to be there. To coerce a child to attend a school where he feels he does not belong will only create resentment.

◆

*One grandfather gave
his granddaughter a car*

for driving to college, rather than trade it in on a new one. He and Grandma didn't need the trade-in value of their older, well-maintained vehicle, and the girl, newly graduated from high school, needed a commuter vehicle.

This can work particularly well if, like a lot of older men, you have learned auto repairs during your retirement years and have maintained the car yourself over a number of years. Have Granddaughter bring the car by regularly. Change the oil for her. Replace the brake pads, belts, and hoses as needed. Don't let the old car become a liability instead of a blessing!

I don't recommend giving a high-school student an auto, though it might be all right to sell them one at market value and with the parents' whole-hearted permission. An exception might be made for an older teen who's shown himself responsible and who is saving his earnings for college.

◆

Consider making your married grandchild's downpayment on a house,

if you can afford it. I think there's a lot to be said in favor of helping your grandchildren avoid a lifetime of servitude to the banks and other money lenders. And while you're at it, here's a chance to show them the huge financial advantage of paying off a mortgage in fifteen years instead of thirty. Remember, mortgage brokers typically use pressure to get young buyers to sign up for long-term mortgages. And first-time home buyers often are incredulous to realize that there's only a modest increase in monthly payments from cutting the length of terms in half.

◆

Help grandchildren over genuine emergencies.

This can range from loaning them your car while theirs is in the shop, to helping with medical bills, or even letting them live in your home.

Again, I would give first priority to children or grandchildren struggling under the often-inadequate salaries paid to Christian workers. A young couple were in their first year teaching at a Christian school when the wife gave birth. This church school's insurance policy fell short, and the couple was left with hundreds of dollars in unpaid medical bills. Another family who live in their home only part of the year allow their married daughter, son-in-law, and children to live there rent free. The father teaches in a Christian school, and his salary is not adequate to pay rent, buy groceries, and put away money for a downpayment on a home of their own.

◆

The principles outlined in 1 Timothy 5:9-10 for aiding only those deserving destitute widows should be applied to your grandchildren.

Grandchildren who are to become recipients of substantial financial aid should have shown themselves responsible in handling day-to-day financial commitments, such as credit cards. And they should have shown themselves generous toward others in need (see Luke 6:38).

Grandparents sometimes have to deal with adult children, who because of selfishness and egalitarian notions of fairness, may expect to see every nickel left by their parents divided equally amongst the children, needy or not, deserving or not. This attitude was expressed in a letter to Ann Landers. The writer complained that "to help one child less than another is a disservice." Said the apparently jealous complainant, "My wife was a victim of such flawed reasoning. Because we had worked hard and were not in need, her father gave large sums of money to his other children." Then the writer offered this advice, arbitrarily restricting his in-laws' generosity: They should have "put an equal amount aside for the others as their inheritance."

The writer's complaint is valid if, as he asserted, his wife's brothers and sisters had squandered their livelihood on "laziness, gambling, and poor judgment." But that is for the giver to decide, not other family members, jealous like Esau or the Prodigal Son's older brother.

Give on the basis of need to those who will use it responsibly. Grandparents who have taught their own children love, sharing, and generosity when they were growing up will not have to face these jealousies later.

◆

If you will have cash and investments left at death,

should you: a. leave it all to your children; b. leave it all to your grandchildren; c. leave it all to the Lord's work; or, d. combine the three approaches?

Counselor Jim Rickard points out that often the grandchildren are in greater need of help than the children, who may be fifty or sixty years old and past their financial struggles at their parents' death. So, "give the grandkids a nudge," based on *need*, he counsels. They may need help getting set up in business, for example.

In the case of a father and son in business together, if the son wishes to continue the family business, make provision so that he will not be financially hurt by his father's death. I've seen too many sons or daughters financially wiped out or left without a needed line of credit, because of the claims of other family members on a family business or farm in which the one in partnership with the parent has made substantial investments in both time and money. Make firm decisions while you're able. Otherwise ungodly wrangling (sometimes by people professing godliness) hurting your family's testimony may continue for a generation or more. In many cases, it is wise to transfer ownership while the parent/senior partner is still healthy and his ability to do so is not in question.

◆

One Christian businessman is giving his
investments to the Lord's work,

and he plans on having his bank account at zero at his death, if possible, tells Rickard. And he's having fun and countless blessing in giving his money back to God, who gave it! This man is truly laying up treasures in heaven.

There is a danger of taking Old Testament passages about patriarchs passing their farms on to each succeeding generation out of context. There is no biblical mandate for such a practice for Christians; this was for ancient Israelites, the people of the land. But common sense should prevail, I believe. Have your children and grandchildren been taught biblical principles of giving, especially those principles relating to Matthew 6:33, "Seek ye first the kingdom of God, and his righteousness, and all these things (food, clothing, shelter) shall be added unto you"? If they have, and they have learned sound financial principles of money management, and if you can leave them enough money to keep them from servitude to the banks, they can build God's kingdom by plowing that money back into Christian service themselves.

But all children and grandchildren, godly or ungodly, ought to have a token remembrance of Grandma and Grandpa, if feasible. I have my Dad's hunting rifle and Grandad's Bible, for instance. An unsaved grandchild may be blessed in later years by a possession which helps them remember a godly grandparent and turn to Christ. A postcard with a motto, crudely hand-framed under a piece of window glass hung on my grandmother's bedroom wall all during my childhood. I found that motto among some of her things more than twenty years after her death, and it is now above my office desk:

"Be Strong! We are not here to play, to dream, to drift;/ We have hard work to do and loads to lift./ Shun not the struggle—face it, 'tis God's gift!"

Though my younger brothers and sisters remember Grandma Wiggin, who died at ninety-five, as feeble and old, confined to a wheelchair, *I* remember her well as the big-boned, strong woman of seventysomething, who though "old" to me, nevertheless worked untiringly at housework and gardening in our Victorian farmhouse, which except for indoor plumbing was little changed from the nineteenth century. It is not the motto that inspires me to go another mile when I am ready to quit nearly so much as the memory of Grandma!

Finally, *consider setting up a living trust, rather than a will,* if you have a substantial estate. This will enable you to continue to give to the Lord's work and to your children and grandchildren while you are living. And under present laws a trust will, unlike a will, enable your children and grandchildren to escape most taxes and probate entanglements on money passed on to them because your assets continue in the trust; only they, rather than you, are now the trustees.

18

Eternal Values

As a small girl my wife, Dot, herself now Grandma Wiggin, often visited her grandmother, who has since gone to be with the Lord. She would hear this dear, uneducated Southern lady from the hills of East Tennessee praying aloud late at night for her children, including Dot's parents, who did not then attend church.

Great-grandma Mary Hackney's prayers were answered. Dot's parents eventually came to follow the Lord, as did their children and grandchildren, most of her aunts and uncles, and dozens of Mary Hackney's descendants, now extending to six generations!

Recently, my married son and daughter were visiting Grandma Wiggin and me overnight with their spouses and children. I led the families in evening devotions, and I asked my son-in-law, the eldest among them, to lead in prayer. I heard his words with interest as he asked the Lord to help him and Mark, our son, to be faithful in their responsibilities as "priests in our own families."

That prayer was a beautiful observation, but it must be understood in the context of Bible teaching. Evangelicals emphasize the individual priesthood of every believer before God, rather than the Old Testament concept of a priest in the temple standing between God and the worshiper (see 1 Tim. 2:5; Heb. 7:23-27, 9:11-15). In Christ's church, therefore, all Christians—men, women, and children—are priests and Christ is our High priest (see 1 Pet. 2:5; Rev. 1:6).

But there is a priestly position within the Christian home, apart from the church, in which fathers are to take the leadership, and grandfathers are to set the example in leading their families in the ways of Christ. There is an example of a grandfather as priest beautifully illustrated in the earliest-written book of the Bible, Job (see Job 1:4-5). Job's married sons and daughters seem to have held birthday parties (see verse 4). But Grandpa Job, knowing the human tendency of even believers in a party mood to forget God, offered burnt offerings, Old Testament fashion, on his children's behalf to God. This is not a suggestion that Christian families return to burnt offerings; rather, the principle is that grandfathers have a priestly responsibility in family worship. In an important sense often overlooked in our day when the value of fathers is downplayed by the media fathers and grandfathers *do* stand as priests between young children and God. The child who does not perceive of his father as loving, for example, may not perceive God as loving, either, and vice-versa.

Moses instructed the people of Israel to "teach . . . diligently . . . your children" the Word of God, and to be so faithful in this that whether sitting at home with the children, or walking along the street with them, God's truth was continually taught the youngsters (Deut. 6:6-9). Moses years later repeated this admonition so that the "children who have not known anything" about their godly heritage might be taught the Bible and the ways of the Lord (Deut. 31:12-13).

Christ gave teachers to "some," Paul tells us, in order that his people might be spiritually built up, that from now on we (Christians) no longer will be "children" (see Eph. 4:11-14). Though "some" properly interpreted refers to churches, "families" will also fit here, for grandparents need to teach their families Bible truth so that their grandchildren may grow "unto the . . . stature of the fullness of Christ" (verse 13).

My maternal grandmother, Grandma Fuller, had been a school teacher before her marriage, and for perhaps a quarter of a century late in her life she was a Sunday school teacher. She was also a teacher to her grandchildren, and when I or my brothers visited overnight, it was her custom to read us a chapter from a child's story Bible and pray with us before bed.

Grandma took this responsibility because Grandpa did not become a believer until we older grandchildren were young adults. We children understood this; at any rate, on Saturday, our usual day at their home, Grandpa was absent during the evening on his duties as a part-time sheriff.

◆

*As a grandparent seeking to strengthen
a grandchild's devotional life, you should build on
the parents' foundation, as much as possible.*

If the parents have laid no foundation, build anyway. I recommend using a child's story Bible for kids under twelve. *365 Children's Bible Stories* by Mary Batchelor (Lion, 1985) is an excellent, heavily illustrated recent resource for reading to all children, and the old standby Bible story books by Hurlbut and Egermier are good, too. For preschoolers try *My Frances Hook Jesus Book* or *My Frances Hook Bible Story Book,* both beautiful books by the well-known illustrator of Northern towels (Standard, 1962). For older children, or for when the entire family is present, read a chapter of the Bible that is easy to understand, followed by prayer requests and one or more family members leading in prayer. For Grandpa himself to lead such family devotions, whenever possible, lends respect and authority to God's Word and the spiritual, eternal values you cherish, I believe.

Jack Wyrtzen, eighty, is a great-grandfather and grandfather to twenty-one, ages three to thirty-three in his family and that of his wife, Joan, whom he married after they both were widowed. And as founder and for over fifty years director of Word of Life International's far-flung youth ministries, Jack is in a spiritual sense no doubt a grandfather and great-grandfather to millions of young Christians around the world.

Yet, despite the heavy demands on their time of the Word of Life ministries, Jack and Joan Wyrtzen try to see each of their grandchildren, except for those in Brazil, "on the average of two to three times a year," says Joan. "They're either here, or we're out there somewhere," she says.

Chuckles Jack, "During the summer they'll all be piling in on us."

I asked Jack and Joan Wyrtzen how a grandparent can pass the eternal values of a Christian heritage on to grandchildren. "I think the greatest thing a grandparent can do is to be involved in their grandchildren's lives," replied Joan. She mentioned that she and Jack have arranged their schedules to attend every grandchild's high school graduation. For example, the Wyrtzens flew to Sao Paulo, Brazil to attend the graduation of Jack's daughter's children. And we "try to call them every week," she said. If the grandchildren are at home, she and Jack talk to them, or "at least we talk to the parents."

Jack Wyrtzen is a letter writer, though he admits he doesn't "get as many as I would like" in return from their grandchildren. But one grandson, in particular, is in college on the west coast, separated by 3,000 miles from his grandparents in Schroon Lake, New York. He was a quiet teen, the Wyrtzens remembered, and he found it difficult to open up and talk. But Grandpa Jack wrote letters to this grandson, and in reply "he just seemed to open up and blossom" in his letters in return, says Joan.

Jack read a portion of this grandson's letter in which he writes, "I really want to thank you guys for all you've done in my life . . . thank you most of all for the spiritual example. I couldn't have had a better example when I was growing up . . . I just wanted to let you (Grandpa Jack and Grandma Joan) know how much I appreciate you for what you've done."

Letter writing has so nearly become a lost art since the invention of the telephone in 1876, it seems, that only a few older grandparents still prefer writing (only 29 cents for a message to be shared and cherished for days or weeks!) to phoning (several dollars a call, if your grandchildren live out of state, for a message often forgotten within hours). My paternal grandparents, for instance, got their first telephone in 1907 when they were both nearly forty, and letter writing was already their established habit. Grandma Wiggin continued to write my aunt until shortly before Grandma's death, though they lived only five miles apart and both had phones. Most American homes had phones by 1950, and personal correspondence has declined sharply since.

So the letters I best remember as a college student were from my aunt, the same age as my maternal grandmother, and from Grandma herself. Grandma Fuller's letters, in particular, were filled with spiritual encouragement and hints of her prayers.

◆

A theme Jack Wyrtzen repeats, both by word of mouth and in his letters to his grandchildren, he says, is "Quiet time, quiet time, quiet time!"

Jack tells, "We keep after our kids—grandchildren, children, all our staff members and everybody else on this theme, because you're never going to be filled with the Spirit unless you're filled with the Word of God."

"The primary function of grandparents," write Stephen and Janet Bly in *How to be a Good Grandparent* (Moody, 1990), is to "pray regularly for your grandkids." The Wyrtzens pray often for their grandchildren, and God's resultant blessing has impressed the Wyrtzen grandkids with the efficacy of Grandpa Jack's prayers. "When my granddaughter called me after her first child was born," remembers Jack, "she said, 'You know, Grandpa, this is the fourth generation—this is wonderful! Pray for my kids, just like you prayed for us.' I think most of our grandchildren feel that way," Jack Wyrtzen added.

The Blys recommend keeping a "picture prayer journal," using a notebook with your grandchild's latest photo, and pages to keep records of birthdays and other occasions requiring special, specific prayer. A purse-sized Grandma's Brag Book, leaving every other page open for a 3 x 5 card for notes, might work for this. Grandpas might use a similar book to keep in their desks. A notebook kept on the shelf with your family Bible makes easy reference for evening devotions and prayers.

So be faithful to maintain family devotions. Your consistent example, especially when your married children visit overnight with your grandchildren, will encourage them to be faithful in family worship also. Pray for your

239

grandchildren. Like Great-great-grandmother Mary Hackney's prayers, or Jack Wyrtzen's prayers for his grandchildren, God will honor these prayers with yet another generation that follows the Lord.

And write often, offering spiritual encouragement. Usually it's difficult to reach college students in their dorms by phone. Younger grandchildren are often not at home when the phone rings. But a letter will get there every time, to be read, reread, and cherished. Hearts will be encouraged. You will be remembered as the grandparent who cared about your grandchild's spiritual welfare.

19

Letting Go without Losing
Your Posterity

Grandpa Wiggin sat down heavily on a chunk of curly rock maple that long ago Saturday morning in January. He pulled a mitten from one gnarled hand and fished a grimy handkerchief from a deep pocket of his mackinaw.

I had not at first been alarmed with Grandpa's coughing and sneezing during the two hours we had spent splitting and stacking stovewood since breakfast. But his coughing had progressed to spitting, and when I saw a red stain in the snow at his feet, I became worried. He rose, and ten more minutes of work with the maul and wedges brought on more violent coughing. "Grandpa, I'll finish the woodpile. You go inside," I finally insisted in frightened exasperation at his determination.

I watched Grandpa's rheumatic hobble as he mounted the shed steps. I took up the sledge hammer, and after splitting half a dozen chunks into kitchen-stove size, I went indoors to check on him. I found Grandpa Wiggin already abed, and Grandma rubbing his chest with camphorated oil. He rose from that bed only once in the three bitterly cold winter weeks he lingered in the warmth of a house he had built himself half a century before, heated by wood he had helped saw and split during the fall and winter months. At age eighty-four, Grandpa Wiggin died on Dad's thirty-seventh birthday, January 30, 1953.

I suppose that my having been with him during his last earthly labors impressed me indelibly with the concept of Grandpa Wiggin as a man who valued hard work. Over the years as I have matured, the impression that incident left on me has a few times induced me to tackle tasks beyond my means (I began one summer between college years driving a farm milk truck, which required wrestling 115-pound cans onto chest-high shelves. After two twelve-hour days, I had to quit). But all in all, far more often it has given me impetus to press on through discouragement to the euphoria of a job well done.

Rarely does a value of a grandparent impress itself into the mind of a child with a lesson as poignant as the death of my grandfather impressed me with the value of work. More commonly, we teach our grandchildren here a little, there a little, leaving marks on their minds and spirits as we interact with them.

Secular psychologist Fitshugh Dodson, writing in *How to Grandparent* (Harper and Row, 1981), has found that the "overwhelming majority" of grandchildren he has dealt with say that they have learned little from their grandparents. Yet I learned much from mine, and if you have a solid relationship with your grandchildren, you can teach them much, as well. For example, I found in Grandma Fuller, a quiet, modest woman who was always courteous and thoughtful, a model of kindness. Grandma Wiggin, a Maine farm housewife from a generation older than my maternal grandmother, was the epitome of frugality, practicing home arts alongside my mother, ranging from canning to soap making to knitting, which kept our large family supplied through long New England winter months. So what if the creamery's check was needed to pay off last spring's seed and fertilizer bill—if we had canned beans and beets on the shelf and bacon and hams hanging on a cellar floor joist, we would eat.

Both grandfathers taught me truthfulness. To utter an untruth was morally abhorrent to them. I remember that Grandpa Fuller, a sheriff, had only contempt for a man whom he'd arrested, then heard perjure himself at a court trial. "The first word that fellow ever uttered was a lie," Grandpa declared.

Grandma Fuller and Grandpa Wiggin were students of the Word. I can still see Grandma preparing a Sunday school lesson for her boys' class as she sat beneath a lamp in her rocker or Grandpa marking his Bible in the glow of a kerosene Aladdin.

◆

Our heritage of American family values has taken a beating during the past half century, and the destructive processes attacking our grandchildren are accelerating.

Strangely, some cultures which do not share Bible-based beliefs nevertheless successfully transmit many positive values of their heritage, such as the careful conservation of cash and other resources, as well as family cooperation in entrepreneurship, to succeeding generations. Orientals such as Korean and Vietnamese immigrants, refugees from two wars, are well known for this. Until recently, crime was virtually unknown among these peoples, transplanted to America.

Though most Japanese young people claim to be agnostics and have abandoned the religious beliefs of their parents and grandparents, social and family traditions are so much more a part of life in Japan than in America that most young Japanese give homage to the old ways, not only in the pageantry of colorful centuries-old dress for special occasions, but in the habits of daily living, as well, reports Paul Horlits, in the ABWE *Message* (Summer 1992). Though not a religion, Confucianism, borrowed from the Chinese some 600 years ago, supplies an unwritten code of behavior on which most Japanese draw for their traditions of social behavior, morality, and family relationships.

American culture is not as devoid of old-fashioned positive tradition based in a Judeo-Christian ethic as news reports, and even many ministers of the gospel would have us believe. Anyone who's spent time in cultures where Judeo-Christian ethics have not been felt, or have been suppressed, such as Africa and the former Soviet Union, can attest to this. In Moscow, for instance, free enterprise, which in the U.S.A., Canada, and Western Europe is accepted as the norm (though heavily taxed!), is slow to catch on. Consumer goods routinely open for free customer inspection in American stores are kept locked behind the counter for fear of theft. Mutual trust, based in biblical morality, has made it possible for Western industry, merchandising, and banking to flourish.

But values which are specifically *family* in nature, such as sexual monogamy, the leadership of the husband-father in the home, respect for elders, and obedience to parents as well as a commitment to Christ and his church rather than the pursuit of pleasure and material goods—these are fast going by the board.

Pastor's wife, mother, and writer Lola M. Williams interviewed Christian men and women, ages twenty to thirty-two, from a wide variety of backgrounds and lifestyles. All had been reared in Christian homes and are all now "serving the Lord in some capacity," she wrote in *Confident Living* (May 1991). Based on the answers to her survey, Williams compiled a report on the common characteristics of these homes where family values and a heritage of Bible-believing Christianity have been carried to the second generation. Though the answers of her respondents are primarily of value to parents, these answers will also prove useful to grandparents seeking to preserve their heritage in their grandchildren. I have extracted ten principles from Williams' article, "Keeping Them in Church," adding some extrapolations of my own:

1. Most successful parents took time to listen to their children, even when it meant putting aside an important task, the newspaper, or a favorite TV show.
2. Parents of Christians who later became church workers took time with each child alone, one-on-one. These children were praised for doing well more often than criticized for making mistakes (see Eph. 6:4).
3. Both parents in the home were united in discipline. One parent would not undercut the authority of the other, leaving the child confused.
4. With small children, the most common discipline used by parents successful in carrying their heritage into their children's lives was spanking; with teens, it was grounding (see Prov. 13:24, 19:18).
5. Eighty-six percent said they had a curfew.
6. The children were exposed to other Christian youth in a variety of circumstances, such as summer camp or a Christian school, in addition to Sunday school.
7. Most such homes had daily devotions.
8. Church attendance was required by most parents unless they were ill. This usually included three

Sunday services and midweek attendance at a prayer service or a Christian children's club, such as AWANA.

9. Sex, religion, and politics were openly, sometimes "fiercely" discussed in many homes. Most children could politely disagree with their parents on such issues. The repressive attitudes which ungodly child experts often claim characterize Christian homes were found in only a minority of cases. Teens were also permitted to discuss their own discipline measures with their parents.

10. Consistency in lifestyle and in dealing with the children, Williams found, was the most common characteristic of a home which saw its values carried on for succeeding generations.

Except in those unusual cases where the grandparents have custody of the grandchildren and can rear them as their own, the grandparents' role is pretty much to be supportive of parents as they seek to implement the principles mentioned above. So "The best thing is to be an example" to the grandchildren, says Grandpa Jim Franks, who describes himself as "The only guy my wife knows who talks back to the television."

"He not only talks to it; he never stops," adds Shirley Franks.

"Why do Hollywood and Broadway deliberately try to destroy family values," ponders Jim, who views much of TV fare as bad examples for kids. And his grandchildren know where he stands on issues ranging from sex to fatherhood, from socialism to the causes of famine in Africa. "I just tell my grandkids it's baloney," he says of anti-family opinions expressed on TV.

"How do you say that without being thought an old grouch?" I asked him.

"I'm smarter than those guys in Hollywood," Jim says, his eyes a-twinkle. "They wind up in the junkyard physically and spiritually." Jim's grandchildren respect his opinions, and they know Grandpa's right.

◆

It's not realistic, of course, to expect your children and grandchildren to copy your parenting practices as if cut out by Grandma's gingerbread-boy cutter.

Nor is it possible. The Franks reared their children in a Christian heritage which shared both Baptist and Christian Reformed evangelical convictions. But one child married a Roman Catholic, and so this set of grandchildren is being raised Catholic.

But Grandma Shirley, who frequently has seen the Lord work in the lives of her children, prayed. And "The priest was saved through the testimony of an evangelical minister," she says. She and Jim went to a granddaughter's first communion at the Catholic church, and "they sang all our songs and the music was Spirit filled," Shirley remembers. "Our daughter loves the Lord, and she prays with her children, and the family studies the Bible together," Shirley says.

Praying with the children, Shirley says, has been passed down through at least four generations. She recalls waking up at night with what her mother called "growing pains"—leg cramps. Her mother would rub Shirley's little legs and pray with her, and they'd pass the time praying for the pain and for family members until the cramps were relieved. Shirley herself passed this practice on to a daughter who also had nighttime leg cramps as a child.

Now Shirley's daughter has a daughter of her own with the same problem. Both mother and grandmother have had sessions with this four-year-old, rubbing her legs and praying for family members. Recently, the small girl was asked to say grace at a family picnic. She prayed around the family circle, remembering aunts and uncles and cousins by name before she finished!

Your grandchildren do not need to be among those in the "overwhelming majority" whom Fitzhugh Dodson believes to be representative of American youth. Rather, prepare Grandma's House for the grandkids. Build Grandfather's Mountain so that, like old Caleb, your heritage can pass on to the third generation (see Josh. 14:11-14).

Grandparents who would hand their heritage of spiritual, moral, and social values on to their grandchildren should consider seriously the words of Paul the apostle to the church in Corinth that Christ "died for all"—grandparents and grandchildren, that "they who live should no longer live unto themselves, but unto (Christ) who died for them, and rose again" (2 Cor. 5:15). This implies that a grandparent should avoid a consumptive lifestyle. I recently saw an elderly, seventysomething couple in a Cadillac, a new one, the big four-door Fleetwood with all the bells and whistles. It never ceases to amaze me that many folks wait until the kids are grown to buy a big, family-size car. What message about life are such grandparents giving their grandchildren?

My kids' Grandpa Hackney, who passed away before the birth of our fourth child, was known by his grandchildren—most of whom are parents themselves now—for his generosity. The neighborhood kids knew him for this, too. He gave away cookies and treats to neighborhood children, who as adults still remember his kindness. And when his own children were young parents struggling with finances, and he and Grandma Hackney—their own kids grown—were both employed, it was often Grandpa Hackney, not mindful of laying up for old age, who sacrificed to buy his grandchildren shoes, socks, winter coats, or school clothes. Like Mary of Bethany, Grandpa Hackney is remembered for his giving heart by several dozen grandchildren, who have become givers themselves (see Mark 14:9).

Read carefully Matthew 6:19-34 from Christ's "Sermon on the Mount." In this passage Jesus contrasts the giving spirit, which lays up treasure in heaven, with the grasping spirit, which seeks to hang on to all it can grab. Verse 33 caps this great message: "Seek ye first the kingdom of God, and His righteousness, and all these things (food, clothing, shelter) shall be added unto you."

As your grandchildren see that your values are eternal rather than temporal, they'll want to emulate you and the heritage you seek to pass on.

Author Maureen Rank, writing in *Dealing With the Dad of Your Past*, (Bethany, 1990), speaks of "launching" one's children "from a childish dependence . . . into a healthy *interdependence*" (italics hers) with others they encounter in their adult lives. Ready for it or not, Grandpa and Grandma, even as our own children grew into maturity and feathered their own nests, our grandchildren will repeat this process, will be "launched" like arrows throughout the wide world (see Ps. 127:4).

We must let them go, releasing them to build their own lives. But can we be assured as they move out of Grandfather's Mountain into the well-watered plains below that they will carry with them the heritage, both goodly and godly, with which we have striven to endow them? I believe we can, as we entrust them into the Lord's care.

◆

For many of our grandchildren now,
and sooner or later for most,
our "most important" responsibility
will be to pray for them daily,
says Shirley Franks.

Grandparents Jack and Joan Wyrtzen and Jim and Shirley Franks attest that God does answer prayer in regard to their grandchildren. Pray *for* them and *with* them, says Grandma Shirley. Later "they can say to their own kids, 'Grandma prayed and Grandpa prayed, so we pray as a family,'" she says.

20

The Grandchild Who Climbs Trees

A small boy many years ago raised up on one elbow in his bed to watch the glow from the grate of an old stove piped into a closed-off fireplace in the master bedroom of a pre-Civil-War-era country inn. The rattle of a stove poker and the squeak of cast-iron hinges had caught the child's attention, and silhouetted in the glow from the stove, an old man in slippers and flannel nightshirt stuffed the stove at the foot of the bed with wood to keep the drafty room cozy against the winds of a northern New England winter night. The old man crawled beneath the quilts on the opposite side of the double bed, and the child, satisfied that Grandpa had not abandoned him to the vagaries of a night in a strange room, fell back asleep. I was that small boy, and the old man was my maternal grandfather, Bill Fuller.

Much is made by some family counselors about parents—and grandparents—telling offspring they are loved. Verbalize your "I love you's." Say it in words—a child needs to be told, we are admonished.

Many children *need* to be told, I'm sure. But I can never recall feeling insecure in the love of either my parents or my four grandparents—not once. Grandpa loved me, though I don't recall that he ever put into words his feelings toward me. He loved me enough to rouse himself at two in the morning to refuel the bedroom stove, and I was satisfied with that!

Like the dog hears "His Master's Voice" from the Victrola in the famous ad, I can hear Grandpa Fuller's voice in the squeak of the door of a century-old stove that sits in my living room. I'm not sure whether the fact that that stove had sat for many years in Grandma's House before it came into my possession has anything to do with it or not!

The influence loving grandparents have on grandchildren is profound, reaching beyond belief. Children need a proper balance of security and daring if they are to become effective soldiers of Christ in later life. My grandparents, as well as my parents, offered me security which I never questioned either as a child or as a teen. They also taught me to climb trees—gave me a sense of daring—both literally and figuratively.

A happy melding of this security and encouragement came in my teens when I helped Dad shingle the back of a three-and-a-half story hillside house. We erected the staging, course by course. As the work progressed, I mounted along with him. Nearly forty feet above a rock-strewn Maine hillside, we stood on a plank catwalk with several shingles just out of reach. I agreed to go up, providing Dad would agree not to let go of the ladder while I nailed the final shingles in place. "Don't look down," Dad warned as I started up. I didn't. And I got the job done.

But not all parents and grandparents are as confident of their children's ability to climb as my dad. Consider the following anecdote, based on fact:

"Jeremy could break a leg!" Eva Jones was emphatic. A grandmother with years of experience in raising children, she felt she had ample grounds to warn Theresa Thompson about her grandson's dangerous behavior.

Theresa explained as patiently as she could that she really *didn't* mind if grandson Jeremy climbed the tall pine in the Thompson back yard near the Jones' property line. "He'll survive—*my* kids all climbed it," she remarked pleasantly as she hung up the phone.

Have you ever wondered why some children become leaders and step confidently out of the family nest to pursue rewarding careers, while others, though they may settle down to a steady job, never seem to rise above the daily routine of running with the nine-to-five herd of wage earners?

Man, created in the image of God, is creative (see Gen. 1:27). He is not bound, like the beast, to his instincts. Yet many folks, even Christians, find themselves forced into such a mold of conformity that creativity is effectively stifled or at least misdirected.

The transformed life of which the Bible speaks seems far from the daily existence of many Christians. "Be not conformed to this world" reads Romans 12:2. This implies, among other things, trusting God to help us break stifling patterns which curtail creativity. And as grandparents, wiser than when we were parents, we must not get ourselves into a rut while guiding our grandchildren. "Don't let the world squeeze you into its mold" is another rendering of this verse.

"Squat down in the trenches. Keep your head low. Don't climb above the level of the crowd," would-be visionaries and winners are constantly warned by the world's various reverse versions of this verse. Grandparents who dish out this type of advice do so at the peril of their grandchildren, who like pinioned Canada geese may never leave the stagnant farm ponds of mediocrity. We want our grandchildren to fly. In God's image, we wish them to climb trees!

Let's take another look at the Jones and Thompson grandchildren. Though the names are fictitious, their circumstances represent several real-life Christian families who have faced very similar episodes in child-rearing.

Eva Jones had had a discouraging time raising her family, and she had had little help from her husband. Her oldest son had not returned to high school after a motorcycle accident had nearly taken his life. It was he of whom she had been thinking when she called Theresa Thompson about her eight-year-old grandson Jeremy. Her next, a daughter, had quit high school to marry, then she had taken a job as a waitress while Grandma Eva tended her two babies. Only her third child finished high school and found a good job.

But her youngest, Susie, still at home and the same age as Jeremy Thompson, was her mother's darling. Susie would never cause her mother concern—Mrs. Jones saw to that. Even as her mother called Mrs. Thompson, Susie had been safely ensconced before the TV filling herself with cookies and Coke while feeding her young mind on a steamy soap opera.

But God wants your child to develop his full potential. Psychologists estimate that the average human being uses only about 2 percent of his brain capacity in his lifetime!

Susie Jones' indolence is apparent to most grandparents reading this. And her mother's indulgence is an all-too-common reaction to the stress of bringing children up in modern times. Our society has gone, within the memory of older grandparents, from a work-oriented culture in which boys and girls had chores to fill their spare moments when not in school, to a leisure-and consumer-oriented culture in which the pursuit of fun and goods fills a child's time and imagination. Many of today's grandparents are poorly equipped to uphold their married children in child-rearing in a society so unlike the one in which they themselves grew up.

Though the drudgery of yesteryear certainly stifled creativity, the vacuum left by the plunge of the American family into materialism is even more deadly to the growth of human potential. But the Christian grandparent enjoys an advantage which grandparents in the world around him do not have. Grandma and Grandpa have in the Bible the resources to help guide their grandchildren to an adulthood which will glorify God. And as the believing grandparent draws on God for strength, his grandchildren will recognize their own spiritual, mental, and physical capacities.

For some grandparents, the directive in Proverbs 22:6 to "train up a child" means merely to take their grandchildren to Sunday school, pray for or with them, and when they are guests in your home, lead them in family devotions. Spiritual training is foundational to the upbringing of children, certainly. But having helped Mom and Dad lay the foundation, these grandparents often expect the child to put up the building of his life with little encouragement other than to warn him with the usual social taboos and moral restraints. Need we be surprised that most adolescents emerging into adulthood build one-story houses—huts even—of their lives, when God's plan is for them to build skyscrapers?

How then can grandparents help their grandchildren build their lives in accord with God's plan? Several principles follow:

◆

The principle of acceptance concerns the fact that God loves us in spite of what we are or do.

A grandparent's responsibility begins with showing the grandchild that he can be "accepted in the beloved" because Christ's death made this possible (see John 3:16; Eph. 1:6).

Children crave acceptance. Your small grandchild will best learn of the Christ who has accepted him as he sees Christ in you. He needs to know, for example, that the paper he brought home from Sunday school is every bit as important as Grandpa's Sunday paper. In terms of the future of his young life, it is far more important. If your grandchildren see that their grandparents are pleased with the small things they shove under adult noses, they'll consider themselves to be of worth before God and before the world. Later, they'll act accordingly, realizing their full potential as adults (see 2 Cor. 5:9). Reinforce their childish efforts by taking that little one on your lap to read his Sunday school stories to him, an act of more value to the child than the content of the paper itself. So what if your newspaper never gets read!

As a child I used to vie with my brother for a turn to sit on Grandpa Wiggin's knee on the way to church in our 1937 Dodge sedan. I recall that I wore short pants and that the car was upholstered in mohair. I'm not sure which was roughest on my little bare legs—Grandpa's wool serge pants draped over his bony knee or the bristly goat hair seats! But sitting there was a twice-Sunday privilege, once coming and once going, and I felt important and loved seated on his lap.

The principle of encouragement
is expressed in 1 Thessalonians 5:11.

To "edify" is to build up. "You can do it, Jeremy," he often heard, both from parents and grandparents. But, "Why bother to try, Susie? You can see that the teacher is playing favorites," was Eva Jones' unfortunate response to Susie's complaints about her school grades. Success in adult life is, I believe, in many ways directly a product of attitudes that one acquires about his abilities while still a child.

◆

The principle of security teaches a child
that God can be trusted to care for his needs.

The secure child will become an adult who can serve God, confident that he'll not be left helpless. Many adults yearn earnestly for the satisfaction of a more rewarding career, only to be held back by childhood-learned fears which make it impossible for them to risk losing the benefits of their present employment. Preferring their retirement pay and guaranteed raises to using their creativity to climb towering trees—with occasional rotten branches—they stick with routine jobs which offer little room for personal growth.

Grandparents who are constantly fussing in front of children about money matters may be damaging their grandchildren's faith in God's loving care. Grandparents and grandchildren should pray together, committing their daily needs to the Lord and thanking him for his blessings (see Matt. 6:25-34). They should provide love so transparent that a child can never question it. My grandparents offered me the security of a love I never doubted as a child, symbolized in my memory by the glow of that old stove's grate and the squeak of cast-iron hinges interrupting the whistle of a northern wind on a winter night.

◆

The principle of self control often must be taught by chastening (see Prov. 19:18).

Jeremy had to learn that lesson. Against explicit instructions not to do so, he spent all the money in his pocket for candy. The "chastening" he received afterward—a spanking by Grandma Theresa and strictly rationed sweets for several days—hurt for a while, but in later life it might save him from financial disaster.

Grandparents should clear disciplinary measures with parents, of course. You can easily alienate a daughter-in-law or son-in-law, or confuse a grandchild, by varying drastically from patterns established at home. While grandparents can teach a parent firm disciplinary measures (How often I've heard a grandmother say, "That kid needs his set-down warmed up!"), sometimes the wisest recourse is isolation or loss of privilege. Grandma is probably not hurting Johnny by giving him two cookies whereas Mom might give him one. But Grandma would surely harm him by letting him raid the cookie jar without correction when he pleases, for example.

◆

*The principle of creativity seems to separate
leaders from followers more than anything else.*

The leader innovates. He dares. He may not have the
inventive genius of an Edison—he may have only the
willingness to try something different at the risk of being
laughed at.

David expressed creativity when he went to meet
Goliath armed with but a sling and stones. Offered the
ready-made armor and weapons of Saul, he chose to use
just the bare essentials (see 1 Sam. 17:38-40). And God
later used David, the innovator, to lead a nation!

Ready-made toys, I think, are often creativity stealing
culprits. Watch your two-year-old grandson become a
highway engineer with a truck, a tiny shovel and a sand-
box—my granddaughter and grandson *both* love to build
things inside the sand-filled tractor tire in our yard! Give
the same child a battery-operated gizmo, and he'll put it
through its paces until bored, then smash it. Why? His
creativity has been frustrated. Destructiveness is nothing
more than misdirected creativity, I believe. Give a child
tools and teach him to build, and you have equipped him
for a rewarding life. Most of the tools in my shop which
I now cherish belonged to my grandfathers—I have
Grandpa Fuller's tool box—and to my dad.

A "best Christmas ever" when I was child was the
year my dad's crops dried up and there was no money
for toys. Dad spent hours for many evenings in the cellar
with his tools. Under the tree on Christmas morning, in

dazzling varnish and glorious red paint, was an assortment of wooden toys, including a kid-sized slide of lovingly planed and sanded maple planks mounted on the frame of an old barrel churn.

Grandpa Fuller spent many hours each day in his woodworking shop behind his country store. Many's the time I've seen him dust the sawdust from his mattress-ticking overalls to slice cheese or bologna. How many of Grandpa's customers may have tasted pine or maple sawdust in their sandwiches the next day?! I learned the joy of following creative urges from watching Grandpa, from helping him assemble a piece of lawn furniture or loading it into his panel truck for delivery. Exactly how much he or my dad, skilled at husbandry, carpentry, and mechanics, added to my urge to create, I don't know. But I do know that watching them, helping them, and enjoying the fruits of their labors gave me a push to try my own creative urges.

◆

*TV is a killer
of creativity.*

The grandparent who succumbs to the urge to let the television set be Grandma's baby sitter is helping that grandchild form a lifelong habit of preferring lazy, vicarious experience as a substitute for real life. With TV, a child doesn't have to think; he just absorbs. With the radio on—remember "Little Orphan Annie," "Inner Sanctum," "Dragnet," or "The Lone Ranger?"—the child's mind supplies the pictures. But with a book, the child must *think,* sort over facts and ideas presented, and creatively furnish his own conclusions. It's no accident that God chose to have his Word recorded as a *written* medium, rather than on video tape!

◆

*Let your grandkids
climb trees.*

In the practical sense, set sensible limits. Children shouldn't be allowed to climb above sidewalks, rocks, or fences, for instance; and such rules will teach them to put realistic limits on the challenges they attempt as adults. Challenge your grandchildren to excel in whatever field they enter. But tailor the tasks you give them to the reasonable limits of their abilities.

"Train up a child" said Solomon (Prov. 22:6). Note the direction. Plants and people naturally, by creation, grow *up*ward. Neither should be constantly beaten down, though both need pruning and direction.

Mrs. Jones, who continually scolded her sons whenever they climbed above their heads, should not have been surprised when, after several years at his job, her third child, the only one who had finished his education, passed up an offer of a managerial position on a commission basis as too risky. Often put down by his parents whenever he sought as a child to express himself, he preferred as an adult a secure, salaried slot in his company. The risks inherent in a chance at greater creativity were too great for a man whose parents and grandparents had failed to build his faith during childhood.

Jeremy Thompson, on the other hand, became an executive with a large, nonprofit Christian organization. His parents and his grandparents are satisfied with their child who climbed trees! Will your grandchildren be among those few who climb confidently over life's difficulties, their eyes fixed on the Son through the leafy shadows of doubt and fear? Or will they remain on the ground, content to nibble on what acorns are knocked loose by the tree climbers? It's largely up to you!